Julia Margaret Cameron

Photographs to electrify you with delight and startle the world

Marta Weiss

Contents

Photographs to electrify you with delight and startle the world

Julia Margaret Cameron in South Kensington

My aspirations are to ennoble Photography and to secure for it the character and uses of High Art by combining the real & Ideal & sacrificing nothing of Truth by all possible devotion to poetry and <u>beauty</u>.

Julia Margaret Cameron to Sir John Herschel, 31 December 1864[1]

Julia Margaret Cameron (1815–79) was one of the most important and innovative photographers of the 19th century. Best known for her powerful portraits, she also posed her sitters – friends, family and servants – as characters from biblical, historical or allegorical stories. Her photographs were rule-breaking: intentionally out of focus, and often including scratches, smudges and other traces of her process. In her lifetime, Cameron was criticised for her unconventional techniques, but also celebrated for the beauty of her compositions and her conviction that photography was an art form.

Julia Margaret Pattle was born in Calcutta on 11 June 1815 (fig. 1), the fourth of seven sisters. Her father was an East India Company official and her mother descended from French aristocracy. Julia Margaret was the most flamboyant of the Pattle daughters, known for their sociability and artistic eccentricity. Educated mainly in France, she returned to India in 1834. In 1836, while convalescing from an illness in the Cape of Good Hope, South Africa, she met the British astronomer Sir John Herschel (1792–1871), who was surveying the skies of the southern hemisphere (p. 107). In 1842, Herschel introduced her to photography, sending her examples of the new invention. He remained a life-long friend and correspondent on technical photographic matters. During the same stay in South Africa, Julia Margaret met Charles Hay Cameron (1795–1880), 20 years her senior, a reformer of Indian law and education who would later invest in coffee plantations in Ceylon (now Sri Lanka) (fig. 2). They married in Calcutta in 1838 and she became a prominent hostess in colonial society. A decade later, the Camerons moved to England. By then they had four children; two more were born in England. Several of Julia Margaret's sisters were already living there, and had established literary, artistic and social connections. Staying first in Tunbridge Wells, Kent, then moving to East Sheen and Putney in London, in 1860 the Camerons settled in Freshwater, on the Isle of Wight, where Julia Margaret later began making photographs. They lived there until 1875, when they moved to Ceylon to be near four of their sons and the family's coffee plantations.[2]

The year 2015 marks the bicentenary of Cameron's birth and the 150th anniversary of her first museum exhibition, held in 1865 at the South Kensington Museum, London (now the Victoria and Albert Museum). The museum was founded in 1852, using profits from the 1851 Great Exhibition, with the aim of educating and

FIG. 2
Charles Hay Cameron, 1871
Carbon print
V&A: 33–1939

inspiring British artists, designers and manufacturers and improving the taste of the public (fig. 3). The South Kensington Museum was not only the sole museum to exhibit Cameron's work in her lifetime, but also the institution that collected her photographs most extensively in her day. In 1868 the Museum gave Cameron the use of two rooms as a portrait studio, perhaps qualifying her as its first artist-in-residence. Today the V&A's Cameron collection includes photographs acquired directly from the artist, others collected later from various sources, and letters from Cameron to Sir Henry Cole (1808–82), the Museum's founding director and an early supporter of photography (See Appendices I and II).

This book, with the exhibition it accompanies, explores the V&A's Cameron holdings. It combines close readings of the photographs and letters with new analysis of archival sources. It draws upon research into the circumstances in which the photographs entered the collection, using untapped sources such as acquisition registers and files.[3] Most remarkably, it reveals that a large group of Cameron photographs in the Museum's collection once belonged to Cameron's friend and mentor the artist George Frederic Watts (1817–1904). This discovery sheds light on previously unacknowledged aspects of Cameron's experimental approach.

Each section of this essay addresses a theme drawn from one of Cameron's letters to Cole. The plates follow the same structure. Cameron's letter of 1865 reveals her early ambition; her letter of 1866 shows her growing artistic confidence and innovation; the letter of 1868 addresses her concerns as a portraitist and desire to earn money from photography, and her 1869 letter describes her struggles with technical aspects of photography. Her final, brief letter of 1872 is that of an experienced exhibitor concerned with practical matters. Together they demonstrate Cameron's development as an artist. This investigation of Cameron's relationship with the Museum and her presence in its collections offers new insight into Cameron's work and career, revealing her to be a bold self-promoter, ambitious for 'fortune as well as fame', but also a self-critical practitioner striving to improve her art.

FIG. 3
Isabel Cowper (1826?–1911)
South Kensington Museum, Educational Collection, 1868–9
Albumen print
V&A: 67559

Cambridge Term divides at Midnight

To Mr Camerons Little Holland House
to have my portrait photographed in her
style: A German Girl held an Umbrella over
me. Mr Prinsep assisting. & the Irish Girls. Saw
Watts who promised to complete his design by 1st
June: Mr Bruces. Museum. Mr Brooke
called & named some of his friends who wd be
likely to give objects :.. Croquet with Hennie &c

20 SATURDAY [140–225]

Museum. Mr Layard, Mrs Bruce, Mrs
Higford Burr - &c to see Cartoons: Board
Robinson most cantankerous: "nothing cd be found"
"Nobody knew of arrangement" - &c. persistent that
he cd only give an opinion by upsetting the arrangement
- R.H. Gardens. very full. In the Ef Mr Ella
came to talk over the Institute Gift. - Closing
of Museum

21 Rogation Sunday — [141–224]

Museum: Art Schools. Accounts. Paris.
Mr Fite came abt Institute Gift. Said "Dont say d
Granville. Say, yourself "which Repudiated.
Thought Fonke a man of Genius - Mr & Miss Marsh
& daughters came to see Cartoons. To Little Holland
House. Met there Sir C. Lindsay & Layard. Mr H. Bn
Home. Sir C L. drove me in his carriage - said
I must have had great will to establish the Museum

Museum. Meeting of R.H. Co: with Fruit & Floral
Committees abt next years Shows: Unanimous
against Saturday. Fr Tues Rate d new. Thurs
Spring d Great — To Musical Co: of S of arts
examined Mr Lucas — Walked with Scott &
Donnelly across the Park - Played at Croquet
in Ef

23 TUESDAY [143–222]

Museum: To Ella's Concert with Hennie
- Met Thackerays there - Walked home
with Annie. - In the Ef went to Ealing
to the Bartleys. - Marian & Fisby then

24 WEDNESDAY [144–221]
Queen born 1819.
Hol at Cm Pleas & Law Offices when kept

returned from Ealing. Museum. with Mr
Bruce & RR on Art Schedule: Mr B. said Robinson
told people that our arrangement was the
laughing stock of Europe! He seemed to think
we ought to take his advice. Lord Granville
hinted the contrary last Board. He doubted
if we shd press him to give list of Spurious &c
- Mr Brooke & Mrs Barnard came to look
at Museum: In the Ef to Mr Gladstones. - met
Milner Gibson & Peto - Mr G said he was my "subject"

From First Success to the South Kensington Museum

I send you my Portfolio...I should be so proud & pleased if this complete series could go into the South Kensington Museum.

Julia Margaret Cameron to Henry Cole, 20 May 1865[4]

On Friday 19 May 1865, Henry Cole noted in his diary: 'To Mrs Camerons [*sic*] Little Holland House to have my portrait photographed in her style. A German girl held an umbrella over me' (fig. 4).[5] Cameron had brought her camera to Little Holland House, the London home of her sister and brother-in-law, Sara and Thoby Prinsep. The couple hosted a regular salon gathered around the artist G.F. Watts, who lived with them.[6] The house attracted Victorian luminaries such as the Pre-Raphaelite artists Edward Burne-Jones and William Holman Hunt, the art critic John Ruskin, writers Thomas Carlyle, George Eliot, William Makepeace Thackeray and Alfred Tennyson – as well as Cole.[7] His brief diary entry forms the first record of the remarkable relationship between Cameron and the South Kensington Museum.[8]

The Little Holland House portrait of Cole is now lost, but another photograph Cameron made there that May includes the sliver of a hand – perhaps that of the 'German girl' – holding an umbrella at the right edge (p. 63).[9] The sitter is William Michael Rossetti, an art critic and brother of the Pre-Raphaelite painter Dante Gabriel Rossetti. In the open air of the Little Holland House lawn, Cameron had less control over lighting than in her glasshouse studio in Freshwater. She made particularly unconventional use of light – an essential component of any photographic process – embracing both extreme highlights and dark shadows. The umbrella would have helped her direct the light as she arranged her compositions.[10] Its presence at the edge of the frame is also indicative of the assistance from others Cameron received, but never explicitly acknowledged.

In May 1865, Julia Margaret Cameron had been making photographs for less than 18 months, yet as Cole noted, she already had established a 'style' of her own. Cameron's story has been outlined many times, beginning with her own account, *Annals of My Glass House*, an autobiographical fragment she wrote in 1874 and which was first published in 1890.[11] Cameron was 48 when she received a camera as a gift from her daughter and son-in-law. She wrote in the *Annals* that they presented it to her in December 1863 accompanied by the words, 'It may amuse you, Mother, to try to photograph during your solitude at Freshwater.'[12] She soon transformed her property to accommodate her new pursuit: 'I turned my coal house into my dark room, and a glazed fowl-house I had given to my children became my glass house!'[13] Although she portrayed the acquisition of a camera as the start of her photographic career, Cameron had compiled albums and even printed photographs before that. She had, for example, given her sister Virginia Somers-Cocks an album inscribed 'photographs of my own printing' at Christmas 1863. She also seems to have collaborated with the photographer Oscar Gustaf Rejlander when he visited the Isle of Wight in the early 1860s, photographing members of both the Cameron and the Tennyson households. On one occasion, she printed one of Rejlander's negatives, surrounding it with ferns to form a photogram frame around the portrait (p. 132). A hybrid work that combines an image made in a camera with a camera-less technique, it shows Cameron's experimental nature and provides a glimpse of her photographic practice before she acquired a camera.[14]

When Cameron did take up photography in earnest, it was arduous and exacting work that involved potentially hazardous materials. She used the most common process at the time, producing albumen prints from wet collodion negatives. The negative was prepared in a darkroom by pouring a solution of collodion – a syrupy liquid made of guncotton dissolved in ether – and potassium iodide on to a polished glass plate. This formed a sticky film over the glass. The plate was then sensitised in a bath of silver nitrate and exposed in the camera. While still damp (thus the name 'wet collodion' or 'wet plate' process) it was returned to the darkroom to be developed in pyrogallic acid, and, to remove any remaining silver salts, was washed and fixed with sodium thiosulphate (also called 'hypo') or cyanide. Finally, the negative was varnished. Positive prints were made by placing the negative directly on to sensitised albumen paper (which used egg white to bind the silver salts to the paper) and exposing it to sunlight. The wooden camera, which sat on a tripod, was large and cumbersome. Cameron's first held a glass plate of approximately 12 × 10 in (about 30.5 × 25.2 cm); her second, which she began using in 1865, held one of about 15 × 12 in (about 38 × 30.5 cm).[15] Each step of the process offered ample room for error: the fragile glass plate had to be perfectly clean to start with and kept free from dust throughout; it needed to be evenly coated and submerged at various stages; the chemical solutions had to be correctly and freshly prepared.

Cameron devoted herself to the medium with energy and ambition. Within a month of receiving the camera she made the photograph she called her 'first success', a portrait of Annie Philpot, the daughter of a local family (p. 51). Cameron later wrote in the *Annals* of her excitement: 'I was in a transport of delight. I ran all over the house to search for gifts for the child. I felt as if she entirely had made the picture.'[16] Sensitive studies of children came to feature prominently in her work.

From her 'first success' she moved on quickly to photographing family and friends, many of them eminent artists and writers. These early portraits include experiments with dramatic lighting, indefinite focus and close-up compositions, all of which would make up her signature style. For example, the portrait of her youngest son, *Henry Herschel Hay Cameron of Charter House* (p. 52) shows her attempting two motifs she would return to repeatedly, the profile pose and the use of strong, directional lighting. By naming his boarding school in the caption she announced his affiliation with a prestigious institution while perhaps wistfully acknowledging that her last child had left home.[17] A portrait of her third-youngest son, Hardinge Hay (p. 53), shows the influence of David Wilkie Wynfield, a painter who photographed himself and his fellow artists in Medieval and Renaissance costume (fig. 5). Cameron corresponded with Wynfield and had at least one photography lesson from him.[18] Some critics at the time compared their soft-focus close-ups. *The Photographic News*, for instance, noted that Cameron's 'style is very similar to that of a series of portraits of painters issued by Mr. Wynfield'.[19]

Among her earliest portraits of literary friends were those of Alfred Tennyson and Henry Taylor (p. 55). Alfred, Lord Tennyson (1809–92) was made Poet Laureate in 1850 and was one of the most famous writers in England. He was also Cameron's close friend and neighbour in Freshwater. Sir Henry Taylor (1800–86) was a well-known literary figure in Victorian Britain and a civil servant at the Colonial Office. When the Camerons first moved to England from India, they became neighbours of the Taylors in Tunbridge Wells, and remained life-long friends. It was Taylor who introduced Cameron to Tennyson. Cameron made at least 32 portraits of Taylor, more than of any other male sitter.[20] He also posed for several of her tableau photographs. Cameron wrote appreciatively in the *Annals* of his willingness to succumb to her artistic demands: 'Regardless of the possible dread that sitting to my fancy might be making a fool of himself, he...consented to be in turn Friar Laurence with Juliet, Prospero with Miranda, Ahasuerus with Queen Esther, to hold my poker as his sceptre, and do whatever I desired of him' (p. 100).[21]

FIG. 5
David Wilkie Wynfield (1837–87)
George Frederic Watts, 1863
V&A: 131–1945

Cameron was extremely prolific during this initial period, establishing the subjects that would occupy her throughout her career, which she classified as 'Portraits', 'Madonna groups', and 'Fancy Subjects for Pictorial Effect'. These were the headings she used on the contents page of an album she presented on 5 August 1865 to the banker and art collector Lord Overstone. Overstone had been a good friend of Charles Cameron at Eton, and gave the Camerons financial assistance.[22] The Overstone album was one of many albums of her own work that Cameron assembled in her first years as a photographer, beginning with one she gave to her friend and artistic advisor G. F. Watts as early as February 1864.[23]

Three photographs of Lady Adelaide Talbot that Cameron made at Little Holland House in May 1865 show Cameron experimenting with portraiture and a 'Fancy Subject', as well as refining the distinctive style that Cole had identified (pp. 60–61). In the most conventional of the three portraits, Lady Talbot sits with a downward gaze in front of a tree. Her hands rest demurely in her lap, one of them delicately grasping a thin branch (p. 60). The half-length pose and sharp, even focus accentuate her dress and ornaments. The close-up profile of the second photograph is radical by comparison and more characteristic of Cameron's pioneering style (p. 60). Here Lady Talbot's head and shoulders fill the frame. Instead of a tangle of branches and leaves, the background is neutral. The focus is soft and the light coming from the right traces the sitter's profile. Although she still does not meet the camera's gaze, she looks to her left with determination, in the manner of many of Cameron's later female sitters. In the third sitting, Lady Talbot appears as Melancholy, the personification of pensive sadness that John Milton evoked in his poem *Il Penseroso* (c. 1631). Draped in a shawl that hides her hair and everyday clothing, her hands are arranged in a dramatic gesture to form a V on her chest. Cameron inscribed the mount of the photograph with two lines from Milton's poem: 'Come pensive Nun, devout and pure, / Sober, stedfast, and demure'. Over the course of her career, Cameron depicted many women both as themselves and playing literary or allegorical roles such as this one. She made comparatively few studies of men in character, preferring a more direct form of portraiture for most of her male sitters.[24]

In May 1864, just months after acquiring her first camera, Cameron began registering her pictures for copyright, taking advantage of new legislation that extended copyright protection to photographs.[25] In the same month, she also began to exhibit her photographs, contributing five works to the Photographic Society of London's annual exhibition.[26] They had an immediate impact. The first critical notice set out the polarised responses her work would go on to attract, and, like many subsequent reviews, noted her sex.

Published in *The Photographic News*, it stated: 'A lady, Julia Margaret Cameron, sends some rather extraordinary specimens of portraiture, very daring in style, and treading on that deba-teable [*sic*] ground which may lead to grand results or issue in complete failure.'[27] Cameron's work was certainly subjected to debate and most of the reviews that followed either celebrated her artistic achievement or condemned her photographs as poorly executed failures.

The harshest criticism came from the photographic press, some of it in direct response to the high praise Cameron's work gar-nered in literary and weekly periodicals such as *The Athenaeum*, *Macmillan's Magazine* and *The Illustrated London News*.[28] *The Photographic Journal*, for example, wrote:

> We are sorry to speak in condemnation of a lady's work; but these photographs have been put prominently forward, and we should be doing an injustice to photography to let them pass as examples of good art or perfect photography.[29]

The disapproval in the photographic journals was so vehement that within a year of the publication of her first review, one critic remarked, 'We hope that esteemed lady has...the hide of a rhinoc-eros – for never has any photographer been subjected to greater criticism than has this lady.'[30] She later claimed to have risen above the attacks, noting that they seemed to have been provoked by the positive reviews:

> The Photographic Society of London in their *Journal* would have dispirited me very much had I not valued that criticism at its worth. It was unsparing and too manifestly unjust for me to attend to it. The more lenient and discerning judges gave me large space upon their walls which seemed to invite the irony and spleen of the printed notice.[31]

Cameron revelled in the praise she did receive, repeating the positive assessments of her supporters in letters and even on the mounts of her photographs, a practice for which she was, in turn, criticised.[32] She also actively campaigned among her more influential friends, asking them to publish remarks in support of her work.

The day after Cole sat for his portrait at Little Holland House in May 1865, Cameron wrote to him, quoting her friends' praise: 'My Dear Mr Cole, I have real pleasure in telling you that Mr Watts thinks my photograph of you "Extremely fine"'. The letter accompanied a portfolio of Cameron's photographs:

> I send you my Portfolio I send you also the framed series for altho [*sic*] I desired Colnaghi to put a copy of <u>Every</u> print in the Portfolio I see some of my very best are missing therefore I suppose he has sold & has no copy left I should be so proud & pleased if this complete series could go into the South Kensington Museum and if you did not approve of this frame you could substitute another at yr. leisure.[33]

P. & D. Colnaghi and Co. was a London gallery, print seller and leading publisher of photographs. Cameron had entered into agreement with the firm within six months of launching her photographic career.[34] The 'complete series', possibly in a single frame, might have been *Fruits of the Spirit*, a series illustrating the nine Christian virtues of love, joy, peace, long-suffering, gentleness, goodness, faith, meekness and temperance, as taught by Paul in the Galatians (5:22–3) (p. 71). It was an ambitious undertaking to try to represent such abstract concepts photographically – *Gentleness* and *Meekness*, for instance, are nearly interchangeable – and even more so to attempt a coherent series of nine. However the fearlessness with which Cameron approached the project, along with the religious subject matter and Renaissance-inspired arrangements of the Madonna with one or two children, make it characteristic of her earliest photographic phase.

Cameron exhibited the entire series at least twice, winning honourable mention for 'grouping and arrangement' at the Photographic Society of Scotland in December 1864–March 1865,[35] and 'for artistic composition' at the Dublin International Exhibition of Arts and Manufacture in May–June 1865.[36] The critics were less admiring. A reviewer of the Scottish exhibition complained that 'with one set of models it is impossible to call up those subtle changes of expression necessary for such embodiments' but found 'the attempt…praiseworthy' and hoped 'to see similar attempts by better photographers.'[37] In the same periodical, a review of the Dublin exhibition criticised the series on religious grounds: 'we can only express our astonishment that any one should suppose himself or herself capable of conveying in a series of photographs, whether bad or good, the full, deep import of the words of Holy Scripture.'[38] Cameron donated a set of all nine photographs, mounted in one frame, to the British Museum in January 1865.[39] Cole, rather than yielding to Cameron's offer, evaluated the works individually, and selected for purchase prints of *Goodness* and *Peace* (under the title *La Madonna della Ricordanza/Kept in the Heart*), choosing the ones that best suited the Museum's needs.

Cameron's energy was remarkable and her dedication to her new medium absolute. In the letter to Cole, her large, loopy handwriting, coupled with minimal punctuation, conveys the breathlessness appropriate to the frenetic pace of photographic activity she described:

> I hope to tone & wash tonight after a day's <u>most</u> arduous work I really fear even my energies breaking down with the work of today. All yesty I took studies of Lady Elcho & Lord Elcho said they were the finest things <u>Ever done</u> in Art! The day before I took 12 portraits and the same day or rather night I printed & I toned & I washed six dozen – therefore I write this word standing midst work. Thank your

Wife & tell her if I had had breathing time I <u>should</u> have enjoyed the kindly proposed soirée.[40]

The letter demonstrates Cameron's hunger for recognition, as well as the extent to which sociability was intricately intertwined with her work and ambitions as a photographer. Her sitters were visitors to her sister's home, attracted by its artistic atmosphere, and many had artistic and literary associations. Lord Elcho, for example, collected Venetian paintings and in 1870 lent 70 works to the South Kensington Museum.[41] Cameron's portraits of Elcho and his wife, along with those of the poet Robert Browning and Sir Coutts Lindsay, artist and founder of the Grosvenor Art Gallery, all taken on the lawn of Little Holland House, were among those later acquired by the South Kensington Museum (pp. 56, 58 and 59). As she did in subsequent letters, Cameron conveyed greetings to Cole's family members along with her requests to have her work collected and displayed by the Museum. Although too busy with her photography to accept Mrs Cole's soirée invitation, she closed the letter with a cheerfully insistent counter-invitation:

> Remember I must see you again & shew you my work before I go.
> Mrs Prinsep says she joins me in the hope that you & Mrs Cole &
> your daughters will come to our shady! Garden here tomorrow
> afternoon
> <u>Yes?</u>
> JMC[42]

Within the next month, Cameron's wish to have her work collected by the South Kensington Museum came true, Henry Cole having placed the item 'Order some Photographs of Mrs. Cameron' on the agenda on 23 May 1865.[43] On 17 June the Museum purchased 63 photographs for £22.4.4 (22 pounds, four shillings and four pence).[44] On 28 and 31 July, Cameron presented another 17 photographs and on 27 September a further 34, bringing the total to 114 (See Appendix I).[45] This was by far the largest acquisition by a museum in her lifetime.[46] Although the second and third groups of photographs the Museum acquired from Cameron were recorded in the Photographs Register as 'presented' (i.e. donated) by Mrs Cameron of Freshwater Bay, Isle of Wight, other archival evidence indicates that the photographs were, in fact, purchased.[47] It is not surprising that Cameron would have wanted to be paid for her photographs. She was extremely generous with her prints, but just as she craved recognition for her work, she also sought to earn money from it.

While the precise circumstances in which the Museum acquired the further two groups of photographs remain unclear, the initial 63 were definitely a purchase. The selection consisted entirely of what Cameron called 'Madonna groups' and 'Fancy Subjects'. All the sitters were women or children, with the exception of G. F. Watts, who posed in one photograph as a male artist receiving inspiration from a young female muse (p. 75). The model for the Virgin Mary in all the 'Madonna groups' was Mary Hillier (1847–1936), Cameron's housemaid and most frequent sitter (pp. 68–69 and 71–73). She posed for the role so often that she became known – at least in Cameron's circle – as 'Madonna Mary'.[48]

The South Kensington Museum thus acquired Cameron's most self-consciously artistic works. These staged and narrative compositions were her most controversial during her lifetime and continued to be dismissed long after. Their critics questioned her use of the supposedly truthful medium of photography to depict subjects such as religious or historical figures who could not have actually appeared before her camera, and accused her of attempting to photograph subjects better suited to painting. Cole's selection of them endorsed Cameron's belief that photographs could take on such subjects traditionally belonging to the realms of painting and other fine art media. For Cameron, however, portraiture was also important, and of the further 51 photographs that she either gave or sold to the Museum, 18 were portraits (pp. 52, 55, 58–60, 62–63 and 128).[49] The remainder consisted of a range of biblical and literary subjects. The later acquisitions not only rounded out the subject matter represented in the Museum's collection of her work, but also brought it up to date by including at least 20 photographs she had taken that summer, some of which were her first attempts with a new, larger format camera.

Details about the exhibition of Cameron's photographs at the South Kensington Museum are frustratingly sparse.[50] An entry for 18 September 1865 in the Museum's register of correspondence abstracts notes that a letter from Mrs Cameron 'Asks permission to exhibit Photos.'[51] By early November they were on view. Cameron's friend Kate Perry wrote to their mutual friend William Brookfield on 3 November, crediting Annie Thackeray, another member of their circle, with convincing Cole to display the photographs. Perry described seeing them with Cameron, whose daughter Julia had been gravely ill:

> Mrs. Cameron looked wretchedly aged, and quite broken down were it not for Annie Thackeray getting Mr. Cole to put her photographs in the K.[ensington] Museum, where she took me to see them. They are very beautiful, and as usual she treats the many-headed monster, the public, as her dear familiar and gossip, writing in large hand on these photographs, MY GRANDCHILD, JULIA MARGARET NORMAN, aged 6, with her nurse, and so on.[52]

Annie Thackeray (1837–1919) was a writer and daughter of the author William Makepeace Thackeray, a good friend of Cameron and her sisters. The Thackerays, who lived in South Kensington, were also close to the Coles, and Cameron mentions them in three of her letters to Henry Cole.[53] Annie published an enthusiastic review of Cameron's photographs in April 1865 and championed her to the South Kensington Museum again on 16 February 1875, when she proposed they purchase 'a book lately published by Mrs Cameron.'[54] The Museum did not act at the time, however, and the V&A only acquired the two volumes of *Idylls of the King*, the book Thackeray was promoting, in 1927 and 1939.

Despite Perry's description, it was in fact Cameron's grandson, not granddaughter, who featured in eight of the photographs in the Museum's collection by the time of her 1865 exhibition. Cameron made numerous studies of her sleeping grandson both as himself and as the Christ child. She inscribed five of the 'presented' photographs of him with variations on the caption *My Grand Child Archie son of Eugene Cameron R.A. / aged 2 years 3 months* (p. 128). When Cameron sent another photograph from the series to Watts (p. 54), he criticised the lack of detail in the cloth covering the child's back and encouraged her to apply higher artistic standards to her work. He wrote:

> If you are going on Photographing your grand child & he is well worth it; do have a little shirt made of some yellowish material, the blot of formless white over the back of the larger boy spoils the whole picture, what would not do in a painting will not do in a Photograph.[55]

With the addition of a small wooden cross and a female model in drapery, Cameron transformed another portrait of her sleeping grandson into an image of the Virgin Mary and the infant Christ (p. 69). The mother leaning over the child prefigures Mary mourning over the body of her son and Cameron called the picture *The Shadow of the Cross*. Cameron often cast a sleeping child in the role of Christ, which had practical advantages, as the infant was less likely to move during the exposure (p. 68). It not only suggested the Pietà, a subject in Christian art in which the Virgin Mary cradles the dead Christ, but also a grim reality for many Victorian families. In Victorian post-mortem photographs, deceased children were often posed to appear as if asleep (fig. 6). In *The Shadow of the Cross*, the framed pictures and curtain in the background reveal the setting to be the interior of a home – indeed Cameron noted elsewhere that she had staged the photograph in her dining room at Freshwater – further blending the domestic and the holy.[56]

Like many of her contemporaries, Cameron was a devout Christian. As a mother of six, the motif of the Madonna and child held particular significance for her.[57] She titled a close-up variation of her grandson and Mary Hillier, in which the figures of the sleeping Christ child and the Madonna nearly fill the frame, *Devotion*, suggesting both Christianity and motherhood (p. 69). On the mount next to the title she added: 'From Life My Grand child age 2 years & 3 months', making the image simultaneously a religious study and a family portrait.

FIG. 6
Unknown photographer
Deceased young girl, c.1845–55
Daguerreotype
V&A: E.637–2014

In aspiring to make 'High Art', Cameron aimed to make photographs that could be uplifting and morally instructive. She was particularly inspired by Italian Renaissance painting, and, as a member of the Arundel Society for Promoting the Knowledge of Art, which published and exhibited reproductions of works of art from the 14th to 16th centuries, she would have seen many important works in reproduction.[58] In some instances Cameron went so far as to attempt photographic recreations of specific paintings, which she described as 'after the manner of' certain artists. For *A Sibyl after the manner of Michelangelo*, she copied the model's braided hair, bare arms and profile pose, with a large book, from Michelangelo's fresco of the Erythraean Sibyl on the ceiling of the Sistine Chapel (1508–10) (p. 77; fig. 7). Cameron would have been familiar with the prints of the Sistine Chapel frescoes that decorated the walls of Farringford, Tennyson's home on the Isle of Wight.[59] She also closely modelled *St. Cecilia, after the manner of Raphael* on Raphael's painting *Ecstacy of St Cecilia* (c. 1513–16), depicting the patron saint of musicians (p. 76; fig. 8). Raphael was particularly admired in Victorian Britain and Cameron would have seen prints and, possibly, photographs of this work. As St Cecilia, Mary Hillier wears an approximation of the dress and headdress as they appear in the Raphael, and holds a wooden prop that imitates the shape of the saint's portative organ.[60] In the original, St Cecilia is accompanied, from left to right, by St Paul, St John the Evangelist and St Augustine, with Mary Magdalene at the far right. In Cameron's version, a man poses as St Paul, complete with sword and scroll of paper, but women stand in for John the Evangelist and Augustine, and Mary Magdalene is left out altogether. Cameron's vision was far too original for even her copies to be literal, and she often cast female models in male parts.[61] For instance, she called a close-up portrait of her niece May Prinsep, *Head of St. John* (p. 92), and for another picture, enlisted a young girl to play Cupid, the Roman god of love, smitten by the beautiful maiden Psyche (p. 84).

The 'Fancy Subjects' the Museum acquired ranged from biblical and allegorical subjects to contemporary genre scenes. *The five Wise Virgins* and *The five foolish Virgins* – according to one critic, all looking 'equally foolish' – illustrate the parable in which ten bridesmaids await the bridegroom, who symbolises Christ (p. 79).[62] The wise bridesmaids, whom Cameron depicts with modestly covered heads and lamps in their hands, keep oil for their lamps in reserve, but the foolish ones, shown with immodestly flowing hair, let their lamps burn out and miss the celebration. Both photographs indicate how challenging it was for Cameron to photograph five models simultaneously.[63] The wise virgins seem squeezed into the frame while the mundane realities of the studio – the glass panes of the roof and the pinned-up backdrop – share the composition with the foolish virgins.

FIG. 7
Giovanni Volpato (1738–1802)
Sibilla Erithræa, after Michelangelo
Late 18th–early 19th century
Engraving and etching
V&A: DYCE.1712

FIG. 8
Pietro Poppi (1833–1914)
Raphael, St Cecilia, Pinacoteca Bologna, 1860s
Albumen print
V&A: PH.3286–1904

Spring, which Cameron set up outdoors, involved only three figures and included a backdrop of foliage appropriate to the picture's theme (p. 83). The critic who wrote of Cameron that 'the staple of her subjects are a lady in night habiliments with a couple of children in a state of nudity' could have been describing it, although the arrangement is similar to that of several of the *Fruits of the Spirit* (p. 71).[64] Cole purchased two variants of *Spring*, one including more nudity than the other, but both representing the season of renewal with a Madonna-like woman and a pair of young girls pressed into a triangular formation (fig. 9).

The triangular arrangement, which was an established compositional motif in Renaissance painting, recurs in *Yes or No?* (p. 81). As in many of Cameron's group pictures, the physical closeness of the sitters, who lean together in a mass of overlapping drapery, conveys an emotional closeness. The two women clasp hands over a folded letter, presumably a marriage proposal, the source of the dilemma suggested by the title. Rather than Old Master paintings, Cameron may have looked to the sentimental genre subjects popular with her Victorian contemporaries as inspiration for this work.

The only published review to note the exhibition of Cameron's pictures at the South Kensington Museum was by the photography critic A. H. Wall, who mentions it in an aside to an attack on her work. After complaining of her photographs' 'clumsily and inartistically arranged drapery, bad pictorial composition, and...palpable distortion arising from a misuse of the lens', he questioned their positive reception in magazines and exhibitions, and wondered at their popularity among the 'higher classes of art-patrons'. He continued:

> I believe I appreciate this lady's pictures at their true value; but of course I may be wrong...I find Mrs. Cameron's photographs awarded a prominent place at the South Kensington Museum close to the picture collections, where they hang 'in their pride alone'.[65]

Wall's critique acknowledges the prestige that a museum exhibition bestowed upon Cameron's photographs. His description shows that, unlike the photographs displayed elsewhere in the Museum as records of faraway architecture or exemplary design, Cameron's were presented as pictures in their own right. Her photographs resembled paintings or drawings, not only because of their Old Master-inspired subject matter and composition, but also because of their relatively large scale, soft focus, and bold lights and shadows. Cole and his colleagues evidently judged that they could hold their own in proximity to the paintings galleries. Cameron's early positive reviews likened her photographs to paintings old and new, invoking artists as varied as Michelangelo, Leonardo, Holbein and Millais,[66] as well as Rembrandt, Correggio and Velázquez.[67] The fact that Cole had eschewed Cameron's

FIG. 9
Spring, 1865
Albumen print
V&A: 44777

portraits of famous men – whose value stemmed in part from the personalities of the sitters rather than the ways in which they were depicted – and purchased (at least initially) only Madonnas and Fancy Subjects seems to confirm that he appreciated her pictures as the works of art she intended them to be. By collecting Cameron's photographs in 1865 and exhibiting them near the paintings, the South Kensington Museum was significantly ahead of its time in its recognition of photography as an art form.

However, Cole also gave four of the photographs he had acquired from Cameron to Godfrey Sykes, a designer then engaged in devising decorative schemes for the building at South Kensington. This indicates that Cole saw them as useful source material for artists and designers. Like most of the photographs by then collected by the Museum, he also saw in Cameron's photographs their potential as teaching tools.[68] In the Museum Register, where the acquisitions were originally recorded, they were listed as 'figure studies from nature' and 'portraits and studies from nature'. At a later date, the mounts of some of the Cameron photographs in the collection were inscribed with the words 'Study for painting'.

Cameron's photographs lacked the clarity of photographs made expressly for the purpose of being copied by artists, such as the studies of trees in winter and summer by Edward Fox that the Museum also acquired in the summer of 1865 (figs. 10 and 11). The tree studies comprised a series entitled, *The Anatomy of Foliage. Photographed examples of the principal forest trees, each taken from the same point of view in winter and in summer; enabling the student to trace the limbs when hidden by the masses of foliage.* Cameron's photographs, by contrast, were plainly artistic interpretations of their subjects and aimed to be works of art. Despite the fact that she often inscribed her photographs 'From life', in the context of the South Kensington Museum's collection, her pictures were comparable not so much to photographs of nature as to photographs of paintings and drawings (fig. 12). Indeed, an 1868 index to the photographs in the National Art Library lists 'Mrs. Cameron' under the heading 'Figure Studies', along with photographs of drawings by Raphael, Mantegna, Millet and Dürer.[69] Cameron herself instructed her gallery Colnaghi's to charge artists half price for her photographs, so even for her, being inspirational to other artists was not necessarily incompatible with being taken seriously as an artist.[70]

The Victorian poet and critic Coventry Patmore, who wrote effusively about Cameron's photographs as artistic achievements, stopped short of declaring them works of art in their own right. Although he wrote that 'the beauty of the heads in these photographs is the beauty of the highest art. We seem to be gazing upon so many Luinis, Leonardos, and Vandyckes', he suggested that

their ultimate purpose was as inspiration for other artists. He maintained that:

> The place of photography is as a guide and corrector of the artist's eye... By the aid of such photography as Mrs. Cameron's, an artist of moderate ability is enabled to produce such portraits as could otherwise be painted by none but excellent artists, and...the excellent artists can arrive at a degree of excellence which has long been regarded as extinct.[71]

In a lecture 'On the Principles of Art as Applied to Photography' George Wallis, Keeper of the Art Collections at the South Kensington Museum, invoked Cameron not as an example for artists to follow, but rather as a model for other photographers. Speaking to the South London Photographic Society on 8 February 1866, Wallis compared the softness of Cameron's photographs to that of Thomas Lawrence's paintings.[72] He advised that:

> Hardness was a fault to be avoided in the photograph, much as in a painting; and this brought him to the question of taking pictures out of focus, for which, referring to Mr.[sic] Cameron's pictures, he thought something must be said.[73]

A. H. Wall, whose low estimation of Cameron many photographic society members shared, 'entirely dissented from the admiration Mr. Wallis had expressed for the works of Mrs. Cameron.' Although 'quite ready to admit that she had produced several most artistic photographs', Wall condemned them as 'out-of-focus' rather than pleasingly soft. Wallis, perhaps cowed by Wall's vehement response, backtracked to explain that 'it must not be supposed that he admired...all [of Cameron's photographs], or defended the haziness by which many of them were characterised.'[74] Nevertheless, it is significant that a senior curator of art at the South Kensington Museum was using Cameron's photographs as a teaching tool within months of their being acquired and exhibited.

Electrify and Startle

I write to ask you if you will...exhibit at the South Kensington Museum a set of Prints of my late series of Photographs that I <u>intend</u> should electrify you with delight & startle the world. I hope it is no vain imagination of mine to say that the like have never been produced & never can be surpassed!

Julia Margaret Cameron to Henry Cole, 21 February 1866[75]

In the summer of 1865 Cameron began using a larger camera, which held a 15 × 12 in glass negative.[76] By early in the following year she seems to have switched to the larger format altogether. In February 1866 Cameron wrote to Henry Cole with great enthusiasm – but little modesty – about the new turn she had taken in her work.[77] Boasting of the originality of her newest series, she now promoted herself in her own hyperbolic language, rather than quoting the assessments of others. Her descriptions evoke powerful physical phenomena: 'photographs that I intend should electrify you with delight', and: 'these great successes have come like meteors out of anxious troubled times!'[78] Along with her ecstatic estimation of her new work, Cameron's letter also betrays a growing awareness of her audience and therefore an increasingly professional viewpoint. She now imagines impressing not just specific individuals, but the much wider audience of 'the world', insisting that 'these wonderful photographs should come out <u>all at once</u> & take the world by surprise!'[79]

Cameron's concern for the approval of certain individuals persisted as well, however, and she wrote, 'Mr Thurston Thompson I hope <u>will</u> be delighted this time.' It is easy to imagine that the Museum's official photographer, Charles Thurston Thompson, whose role was to create record photographs of works of art and architecture, as well as to instruct members of the Royal Engineers in photography, would have prized technical precision and therefore been critical of Cameron's work. Whether or not he was delighted by the works she sent in 1866, by 1867 he was reporting from the Paris International Exhibition, where her portrait of Sir John Herschel was awarded honourable mention, that 'Mrs. Cameron shows many of her admirable works, full of artistic feeling and refinement.'[80]

With her new camera, Cameron initiated a series of large-scale, close-up heads. These fulfilled her photographic vision, a rejection of 'mere conventional topographic photography – map-making and skeleton rendering of feature and form' in favour of a less precise but more emotionally penetrating kind of portraiture (pp. 89–96).[81] She also continued to make narrative and allegorical tableaux, which were larger and bolder than her previous efforts (pp. 97–101).

A comparison of two versions of *Sappho*, made about six months apart, illustrates the evolution of Cameron's style as she moved to the larger format camera (figs. 13 and 14).[82] Mary Hillier plays Sappho in both versions, wearing the same necklace of lockets and very similar embroidered jackets. In the first photograph, details such as the prop lyre, the ivy-covered background and a glimpse of the chair on which Hillier is seated, ground the photograph in its own time and place. This is a photograph of a model dressed up as the ancient Greek poet in Victorian England. The second, larger photograph emphasises the woman herself. Without the accompanying prop, the patterned jacket functions less as a costume than as a formal counterpoint to the simplicity of the composition. Although Hillier's dark hair nearly merges with the plain dark background, her profile stands out dramatically. This Sappho is strong, heroic and timeless. Cameron was clearly pleased with the second image since she printed multiple copies, despite having cracked the glass negative.

In the 1866 letter, Cameron refers to a 'new series of 12', which may have been the group of 12 photographs she listed under the heading 'Series of Life-sized heads of fancy Subjects' in an 1868 priced catalogue of work for sale at the German Gallery in New Bond Street.[83] Most of these were intended neither as portraits of the individuals nor as specific characters; they were simply artistic studies, rendered with intensity and tenderness. A close-up of Alice Keown, whose father was a military officer stationed on the Isle of Wight, simply called *Alice*, was number six on the list (p. 94).[84]

Cameron wrote that if Cole was interested she would 'answer at once by sending [him] the supply'. The Museum did not acquire any more works by Cameron at the time – or indeed during her lifetime – but according to two entries in the Museum's correspondence abstracts she did offer some: on 26 February 1866, Mrs Cameron 'Sends 13 photos for receipt as gifts or loans', and on 11 April 1866, she 'Forwards photographs'.[85] Twelve of the photographs that Henry Cole's son, Alan, donated to the Museum in 1913 date from late 1865 and 1866 and are some of the earliest works Cameron made with her new camera.[86] Alan Cole had begun working at the Museum in 1863 and was acquainted with Cameron, who mentions him in several of her letters to Henry Cole.[87] So it is possible that the photographs Cameron sent in 1866 somehow ended up in Alan Cole's possession, either at the time or by inheritance from his father (see Appendix I). The four photographs that Cameron mentions in her 1869 letter to Henry Cole were also donated by

FIG. 13
Sappho, 1865
Albumen print
V&A: 44753

FIG. 14
Sappho, 1865
Albumen print
V&A: 947-1913

Alan Cole, which suggests that either father or son also kept them at the time.[88] Although the exact movements of the prints remain unclear, it would appear that they crossed the blurred boundaries between Henry Cole's personal and professional lives, just as Cameron blended the two in her photographic career.

When Cameron showed her new photographs at the Exhibition Soirée of the Photographic Society on 7 June 1866, they commanded at least some of the attention she believed they deserved. *The Photographic News* reported:

> Perhaps most striking amongst the novelties, and certainly amongst the contributions exciting the most attention, were the pictures of Mrs Cameron, many of which were nearly life-sized heads, which were stated to have been taken direct, without enlargement.

Indeed, Cameron inscribed many of her mounts from this period with statements such as 'From life not enlarged'. The review praised the work in comparison to her earlier efforts, noting,

> Some of the large heads...were exceedingly charming, and possessed artistic qualities rarely seen in photographs...Some profile heads were also very fine, and free from the blurred contours and smudgy gradations we have before condemned.[89]

The British Journal of Photography was also complimentary, but grudgingly so, conceding that 'this lady seems to be acquiring facility in manipulation, her pictures being much more perfect in the photographic technicalities than when we last had occasion to notice her works.'[90]

One of the works she exhibited was *Beatrice* (p. 89). The source for the image of a white-turbaned young woman looking mournfully over her shoulder would have been instantly recognisable to Cameron's audience as a painting of Beatrice Cenci by Guido Reni. Beatrice Cenci was the tragic heroine of a true story: in 16th-century Rome, she had her abusive father murdered and was then executed along with her conspirators. Although the painting, in the collection of the Palazzo Barberini in Rome, is now believed to represent a sibyl or prophetess and is no longer attributed to Reni, in the 19th century it inspired Shelley's poetic drama *The Cenci* (1819), featured in Nathanial Hawthorne's novel *The Marble Fawn* (1860), and was reproduced in various media (figs. 15 and 16).[91] Cameron made seven variations of her niece May Prinsep as Beatrice, including one with her eyes down (fig. 17), which she later advertised as part of her series of life-sized heads, along with the 'eyes open' version (p. 89).[92] She called some of the other versions *A Study of the Cenci*, and used that title again when she revisited the subject, using Alice's sister, Kate Keown, as the model, in 1868.[93] All but one of the eight versions show the model gazing over her right shoulder, while in the original, Beatrice looks over her left shoulder. This suggests that Cameron used a reversed print of

the original as her inspiration.⁹⁴ A possible source is the print of Beatrice after Guido Reni published in London 1834 in *Lives and Portraits of Celebrated Women of all Countries* by The Duchess of Abrantes (fig. 18). The volume was advertised in journals such as *The Spectator* and *The Athenaeum* and promised to establish for celebrated women:

> a Pantheon, where they shall again live in their genius, their virtue, their talents, their services, and even their crimes, whatever the latter, by a mixture of greatness and of energy, rise above the common standard, and form part of an extraordinary life worthy of being placed under the eyes of generations to come.⁹⁵

Although there is no evidence that Cameron consulted *Lives and Portraits of Great Women*, or any of the other reversed prints in circulation, it is appealing to imagine her doing so. In any case, Beatrice Cenci was part of the pantheon of strong women (both real and fictional) that Cameron created in her photographs. These included, among others, the poet Sappho (pp. 74 and 91), the biblical Queen Esther (p. 100), the philosopher Hypatia (p. 104) and the Arthurian enchantress Vivien (p. 119).

When Cameron exhibited *Beatrice* subsequently it attracted mixed reviews. *The British Journal of Photography* objected to a photograph inscribed 'from the life' representing a long-dead historical figure, and sarcastically remarked, 'we shall...assume that photography is of an older date than we give it credit for'. Never missing a chance to criticise Cameron's technique, the review concluded, 'we must in all candour admit that the art has made immense strides since the day when Signora Cenci submitted her face to the gaze of Mrs. Cameron's lens.'⁹⁶ For the *Photographic News* reviewer, Cameron's version suffered by comparison to the famous painting:

> It is a somewhat dangerous thing to suggest comparisons, and when we find a female head, turned over the shoulder, with white turban headdress, described as 'Beatrice', the mind involuntarily reverts to the touching beauty of a face, with eyes in which a strangely wistful look of tenderness and sorrow are blended, which is known as Guido's portrait of Beatrice Cenci. And the photograph of the pleasing face, with nothing of the rare beauty, and still less the wondrous expression, in the historical portrait, will not satisfactorily bear the comparison.⁹⁷

Making such a clear reference to a well-known painting invited criticism of Cameron's artistic ambitions for photography. According to another review, which began, '"Beatrice Cenci" we like best', Cameron's soft-focus technique – 'rich in suggestion, but defective in execution' – suited the subject matter: 'the low tone and absence of crispness and vigour combine with the pensive sweetness of the expression of the original picture, considerably more...than a sharp, vigorous, well-made portrait of the model could possibly have done.'

FIG. 17
Beatrice, 1866
Albumen print
V&A: 945–1913

FIG. 18
François Le Villain (active 1820s–30s)
Beatrix Cenci, 1833
From The Duchess of Abrantes, *Lives and Portraits of Celebrated Women of all Countries* (London 1834), opposite p.17
Lithograph
V&A: NAL 100.J.4

The author continued, however,

> It is very doubtful...whether this is the legitimate province of photography. The great triumph of the art consisting in its marvellous rendering of details, in which it transcends human skill, to employ it in producing suggestive sketches which a painter can produce better, and quite as easily, is almost as logical as employing a steam-engine to draw a cork or thread a needle.[98]

Although the reviewer was initially seduced by the picture, its resemblance to a painting all too easily led back to the argument about photography overstepping its claim as an art form by attempting to do what painting could do better.

Cameron's staged groups were even more controversial than her depictions of individual characters. Some critics, such as the *Morning Post* reviewer of Cameron's 1868 exhibition at the German Gallery praised them with comparison to Old Master painting:

> Besides the portraits we have an interesting collection of fancy-figure subjects, taken from the life, but draped in classic costume, and grouped with Raphaelesque grace, so as to resemble some of the scriptural or allegorical studies of the old masters.[99]

But most critics were less lenient. Even some of Cameron's most vocal supporters admired her portraits but dismissed her staged photographs as overly theatrical or as misguided attempts to imitate painting.[100] An otherwise positive review of the German Gallery exhibition noted that 'some of the groups or tableaux vivants lose, from the very reason of their artificialness, that noble and natural harmony of expression which is the charm of Mrs. Cameron's productions'.[101] Coventry Patmore, who championed Cameron's portraits, criticised her for 'endeavour[ing] to make pictures out of them'. He complained:

> She is not content with putting one or more noble heads or figures on her paper; but she must group them into tableaux vivants, and call them 'Faith, Hope, and Charity,' 'St. Agnes,' 'The Infant Samuel', 'The Salutation, after Giotto', &c. &c. The effect of this is often strange, and sometimes grotesque'.[102]

Unsurprisingly, the photographic journals were even more damning:

> ...for the so-called art photographs it is impossible to find any terms of praise. They are weak and thin: the fancy in them is of the most mechanical; and the compositions show claptrap and *pose plastique* of the most wooden type...The absurdity of making ideal subjects out of *materiel* which admit no more use of any artistic faculty than the arrangement of a child's doll-house or rockwork for an artificial cascade does not seem ever to have appeared to the photographer of these unfortunate works. To expend serious criticism on them is a waste of words.[103]

Cameron's most sustained effort at staging photographs were her illustrations to Tennyson's *Idylls of the King*, his series of narrative poems based on the legends of King Arthur. Cameron made the photographs at Tennyson's invitation, but when only three of her large photographs were published as small, wood-cut copies, she decided to produce her own edition. In Cameron's version, she accompanied original photographic prints with extracts from the poems, written in her own handwriting, and printed in facsimile (pp. 116–123). She claimed to have made as many as 245 exposures to arrive at the 25 she finally published in two volumes entitled *Illustrations to Tennyson's Idylls of the King and Other Poems* in 1874 and 1875.[104] The illustrations ranged from intense studies of individual characters, such as King Arthur (p. 115) and the May Queen (p. 121) to more fully realised narrative scenes. In *Vivien and Merlin*, Vivien, played by Agnes Mangles, casts a spell over the wizard Merlin, played by Cameron's husband Charles (p. 119). Mangles later wrote that Charles could not stop chuckling during the sitting, thus spoiling many negatives.[105] The makeshift costumes, backdrops and props Cameron used evoke the amateur theatricals and tableaux vivants that were popular in Victorian Britain.[106] The most theatrical of Cameron's illustrations to the *Idylls* is *The Passing of Arthur*, in which the wounded King Arthur is taken by boat from Camelot (p. 123). Cameron used fabric to create the illusion of waves and mist, and even drew a moon on the negative in the upper left corner. *Illustrations to Tennyson's Idylls of the King* was Cameron's most commercially ambitious project, but it was ultimately unprofitable. It was perhaps the culmination of her efforts to earn money from photography, which is the subject of the following section.

Fortune as well as Fame

...thro your gracious loan of those two rooms I am likely now to acquire fortune as well as fame, for...a woman with sons to educate cannot live on fame alone!

Julia Margaret Cameron to Henry Cole, 7 April 1868[107]

When Cameron photographed her intellectual heroes such as Tennyson, Herschel and Taylor, her aim was to record 'the greatness of the inner as well as the features of the outer man'.[108] Another motive was to earn money from prints of the photographs, to help alleviate her family's financial troubles, caused in part by the failure of coffee crops in Ceylon. The subjects of many of Cameron's 'out-of-focus portraits of celebrities', as *The Photographic Journal* put it, were members of her social circle, and some were her close friends.[109] She also sought out sitters precisely because of their celebrity and used autographs to increase the value of some portraits.

Despite the aim of gaining income from the sale of her photographs, Cameron's motivations were distinct from those of a studio photographer who made portraits of customers to order. Cameron stated this clearly in the *Annals*, through a mocking account of a 'Miss Lydia Louisa Summerhouse Donkins', who mistook Cameron for just such a commercial photographer. After quoting the woman's letter assuring Cameron that she is a 'carriage person' and would therefore 'arrive with her dress uncrumpled', Cameron wrote:

> I answered Miss Lydia Louisa Summerhouse Donkins that Mrs. Cameron, not being a professional photographer, regretted that she was not able to 'take her likeness' but that had Mrs. Cameron been able to do so she would have very much preferred having her dress crumpled.[110]

Cameron was making both a social and an artistic statement. By distinguishing herself from a commercial photographer, she emphasised her higher social standing over someone who took pictures for a living. Judging from her condescending tone, she also considered herself to be of a higher social class than Miss Lydia Louisa Summerhouse Donkins. Cameron's preference for a crumpled dress further distanced her from ordinary studio photography and underscored her unconventional sense of what makes a beautiful picture. If Cameron's practice was unlike that of studio photographers who made a living from photography, it was also unlike that of the amateur photographers of her time, who could afford to make artistic photographs without hoping (or indeed, desiring) to earn any money. By positioning her work in a public collection and exhibiting it in commercial galleries, while aiming to make photographs of the highest artistic value, Cameron's ambitions were very much like those of professional art photographers today.

In January 1868, Cameron opened a large solo exhibition at the German Gallery in New Bond Street. A critic writing for *The Standard* was impressed by her technique, but credited the success of her most interesting portraits to Cameron's discerning taste and social connections:

> The portraits are...remarkable for force and tenderness of expression and a classical effectiveness never attained in photographs before. Mrs Cameron has had the taste and judgment to choose persons of noble appearance. The male heads are of the noblest type of intellectual beauty, and she enjoys the advantage of being able to influence some of the most illustrious authors and artists of the age to take a seat before her camera...so that her photographic portraits have a distinguished interest for the public.[111]

In March 1868, Cameron's personal connections with Henry Cole facilitated her use of two rooms at the South Kensington Museum as a portrait studio.[112] Moving her photographic operations to the South Kensington Museum was a significant undertaking, and Cameron probably did it in the hope that it would be financially worthwhile. In her letter of thanks to Cole, Cameron mentions some of the sitters she has photographed already and asks for help securing more, including, she writes hopefully, any 'Royal sitters you may obtain for me'. The letter makes clear her commercial aspirations, detailing the photographs she had sold:

> Mr Spartali was a most glowing & enthusiastic admirer of my works with a very graceful note of thanks he gave me an order for 40 copies of his daughter's pictures enclosing a cheque for [Cameron's strikethrough] 20 guineas –
> Mr Dan Gurney an order for 24 – with a cheque for £12.10.[113]

Michael Spartali was the Greek consul in London and Cameron photographed his daughters Christina and Marie at the South Kensington Museum.[114] Marie was a painter and artist's model, and also posed for Cameron in costume while visiting Freshwater in the summer of 1868. There, Cameron cast her as Hypatia, a 4th-century Greek philosopher in Alexandria, one of the many strong women Cameron depicted (p. 104). Cameron seems to have photographed the banker and antiquarian Daniel Gurney, who was the father-in-law of one of her nieces, at the South Kensington Museum,[115] but it is not clear whether the 24 prints he ordered were of his own portrait. In the letter to Cole, the important point for Cameron was that she had sold her photographs. Her concluding lines betray some of the anxiety she was feeling regarding her

FIG. 19
Henry Cole, c. 1868
Albumen print
Royal Society of Arts, London

FIG. 20
Charles Roberts (active 1870–1898)
Henry Cole, Esq., C.B., after Julia Margaret Cameron
From *The Graphic*, 16 May 1871, p.420
Engraving
V&A: NAL PP.8.D-E

family's precarious finances: 'all this I tell you to show you that thro your gracious loan of those two rooms I am likely now to acquire fortune as well as fame, for as I told you and you gave me entire sympathy a woman with sons to educate cannot live on fame alone!'[116]

Cameron photographed Henry Cole again during her residency at the Museum. On 14 March 1868 he noted in his diary: 'Museum: After lunch with Mrs. Cameron who took six negative portraits of me.'[117] The resulting portrait is the only surviving portrait of Cole by Cameron, and is now in the collection of the Royal Society of Arts (fig. 19).[118] Only one print of the photograph is now known, but the portrait was reproduced as an engraving and widely circulated in illustrated periodicals such as *The Illustrated London News* and *The Graphic*, where the original photograph was credited to 'Mr. Cameron' (fig. 20).

In addition to the transactions Cameron reported to Cole, she sought further sales by immediately marketing some of the portraits she made at the Museum. On Wednesday 18 March, the German Gallery advertised that her exhibition had been extended to the following Sunday, adding: 'This last week Mrs Cameron will exhibit an entirely new series of Photographs, chiefly portraits taken during this month, and to be published at the Gallery This Day (Wednesday), the 18th, and succeeding days.'[119] A copy of the exhibition's priced catalogue, annotated by Cameron, is now in the National Media Museum. Some of the handwritten additions are portraits she made at the South Kensington Museum, including *Joachim*, priced 12 shillings 6 pence, and *Miss de Fonblanque*, priced towards the upper end of Cameron's scale at 16 shillings, the same as *Beatrice* or a portrait of Herschel without his signature (prints signed by him were more expensive).[120] Cameron made at least five variations of the violinist Joseph Joachim (1831–1907), with and without his instrument.[121] She photographed Louise Beatrice de Fonblanque (dates unknown), a young woman known at the time for her beauty, in her own clothes[122] and draped in a manner similar to Cameron's depiction of Beatrice Cenci (p. 89), perhaps as a play on the sitter's middle name. She inscribed one, 'From life taken at the South Kensington Museum, March 1868' (p. 103) and added a similar inscription to one of the prints of Joachim (fig. 21). Cameron might have thought that the Museum's name would enhance the value of the prints, or at least boost her own status by association with the cultural institution.

Another title Cameron added by hand to the German Gallery price list was *Spear or Spare*, priced at 16 shillings (p. 113).[123] Evidently she was hoping to capitalise on public interest in the Abyssinian Expedition, a conflict involving British forces in what is now

Ethiopia, when she photographed Prince Dèjatch Alámayou, the seven-year-old orphaned son of the Ethiopian emperor Tewodros II (Theodore), and his guardian, Captain Tristram Speedy, to whom the emperor had given the Amharic name Báshá Félika, in July 1868 (pp. 112–113). Tewodros had committed suicide rather than surrender to the British; his wife died soon afterwards. Their son came to live on the Isle of Wight and Queen Victoria took a special interest in him, paying for his education and allowing him to be buried in Windsor Castle when he died of pleurisy, aged 18.

In Cameron's portrait, he appears forlorn, wearing Abyssinian dress and in front of a shield, with a white doll balanced in his lap (p. 112). In *Spear or Spare* Captain Speedy is posed in Abyssinian costume for a threatening tableau with the prince's attendant. Cameron's gallery placed a long advertisement promoting the photographs in triumphalist terms:

> Now Published, at Messrs Colnaghi's a series of most interesting Historical and Pictorial Photographs, by Mrs. Cameron, from the life, of King Theodore's son Detach Alamayou and Basha Felika. These portraits are taken in full Abyssinian costume. The young prince is represented under the guardianship of England, personified by the heroic form of Captain Speedy, which the far-famed shield, the many-ribbed sword – each silver rib denoting a victim slain – the lion skin, and other Abyssinian trophies, give every interesting feature to the picture.
> To those who know Mrs. Cameron's Photographs it is enough to say that these portraits of King Theodore's son rank among her very best.[124]

Earlier that month, the South Kensington Museum had opened an exhibition of 'Abyssinian objects from the Emperor Theodore, Lent by the Queen, the Admiralty and others.'[125] Cameron also photographed General Robert Napier,[126] who led the Abyssinian Expedition, and it is tempting to believe she made the portrait during her time at the South Kensington Museum. Regardless of where she photographed Napier, Cameron's photographs of figures associated with British–Abyssinian affairs demonstrate not only her commercial ambitions, but also, as someone who had spent much of her life in outposts of the British Empire, an acceptance of British colonialism consistent with her own affiliations.[127]

Her Mistakes Were
Her Successes

Mrs. Cameron...was the first person who had the wit to see her mistakes were her successes, and henceforward to make her portraits systematically out of focus.

Coventry Patmore, *Macmillan's Magazine*, January 1866[128]

Lack of sharp focus was a fundamental feature of Cameron's photographs, and the subject of much comment among her contemporaries. In 1874 she gave her own, retrospective account of the discovery of her most noteworthy technique:

I believe that what my youngest boy, Henry Herschel...told me is quite true – that my first successes in my out-of-focus pictures were a fluke. That is to say, that when focusing and coming to something which to my eye, was very beautiful, I stopped there instead of screwing the lens to the more definite focus which all other photographers insist upon.[129]

Although Cameron stated that she began making 'out-of-focus pictures' as a 'fluke', she immediately contradicted herself with an account of her highly controlled process of focusing until the picture looked beautiful. On the one hand she seemed to deflect credit for the discovery, while on the other, she described a conscious rejection of 'the more definite focus which all other photographers insist upon' in favour of what she found beautiful.

The words 'fluke', 'mistake', 'accident' and 'chance' recur in the contemporary criticism of Cameron's photographs. The meanings of the terms differ, but collectively they imply a lack of agency on Cameron's part. This relates both to her status as a woman and to her technique, which was alternately praised for its artistry and attacked for its 'slovenliness'. Like Cameron's initial review, the first words of which were, 'A lady', many later notices mentioned Cameron's sex, sometimes in passing, but frequently in patronising terms.[130] Some authors thinly veiled their condescension with apologies including, 'We are sorry to have to speak thus severely on the works of a lady...'[131] or supposed self-restraint such as, 'it would be ungallant to say more in this strain'.[132] Others were more blatantly sexist; one critic wrote: 'For Mrs. Cameron's heads there must be some excuse made for their being the work of a woman; but even this does not necessitate such fearlessly bad manipulation.'[133] Even when critics did not explicitly mention the fact that Cameron was a woman, their comments regarding her technical competence (or lack of it) carried gendered implications. The reference to her techniques as accidental – both by Cameron herself and her critics – perpetuated an image of a female practitioner who only managed to make good pictures by chance. The letters and photographs in the V&A's Cameron collection, however, demonstrate that she was ambitious, hard working, discerning, and constantly striving to improve.

Supporters as well as detractors promoted the notion that Cameron's distinctive style had been derived by mistake. Coventry Patmore was perhaps the first to suggest it, in 1866, when he declared that Cameron was 'the first person who had the wit to see her mistakes were her successes, and henceforward to make her portraits systematically out of focus.' The idea was repeated by a reviewer in *The Times* the following year:

> Her process is stated to be the result of an accident. She happened to use a small lens to produce a large work. The result was that the hardness of outline for which most of our photographers are remarkable was effectually avoided. The lens could not do what the lady wanted it to do, and so produced an image with a blurred delineation; so she strives for this blurred effect, and in many cases succeeds in turning out a head with a good deal of power in it, and with a softness of outline which is in singular contrast to the ordinary style of photographs.[134]

Other admirers of Cameron's work detected an appealing lack of literalism and certainty in the pictures themselves and praised 'Mrs. Cameron's mechanism' for yielding 'results that are at once beautiful and uncertain and which appeal to the imagination, for they are alive with a natural spirit of life and chance and grace and power'.[135] A. H. Wall, on the other hand, used the concept of chance to undermine Cameron's efforts, writing, 'Some of Mrs. Cameron's productions are undoubtedly beautiful; but if these were not obtained by chance, but by design, why are they not more common?'[136]

Few critics actually credited Cameron with mastery over the medium. The author of a review in *The Morning Post* did, enthusing:

> Mrs. Cameron has carried the art of photography to a more poetic degree of perfection than any other photographer whose works have come under our notice. No other artist with whom we are acquainted has combined with such absolute mastery over the technic resources of the art so refined a taste and so large an amount of genuine artistic feeling.[137]

A review in *The Standard* also cited control rather than accident as the source of Cameron's artistry:

> The objectionable hardness common in photographs is entirely unknown in the production of this lady, who has acquired a control over the lens which is very remarkable. Some of the impressions are little inferior to good mezzotint engravings after the original portraits of Sir Joshua Reynolds.[138]

The blurriness of Cameron's photographs could be caused by the lens not being sharply focused or by the movement of the sitter during the relatively long exposure time (or both).[139] Those who admired her work saw her use of soft focus as artistic and painterly, in contrast to the overly literal and mechanical results they perceived in other photographs. These supporters, writing mainly in the non-photographic press, praised Cameron for showing how artistic photography could be. They admired not only her photographs' resemblance to paintings and drawings, but also that their haziness left aspects of the pictures to the imagination. Cameron's good friend Annie Thackeray had eloquently described the virtues of Cameron's technique in an unsigned article in the *Pall Mall Gazette* in 1865, contrasting it with the sharp precision that was the aim of the popular studio portraitist:

> It is, perhaps, no disparagement to Mrs. Cameron to say that she is *not* a popular artist… People like clear, hard, outlines, and have a fancy to see themselves and their friends as if through opera-glasses, all complete, with the buttons, &c., nicely defined. These things Mrs. Cameron's public may not find, but in their stead are very wonderful and charming sights and suggestions… A well-known photographer said the other day, that hers was the real and artistic manner of working the camera; that he, too, had tried to photograph 'out of focus', as it has been called, but the public would not accept it, and he had therefore been obliged to give it up.[140]

Thackeray assumed that 'the public' would reject Cameron's photographs, but it was the photographic community that objected to them most vehemently. Cameron's detractors detected in her work a basic misunderstanding of the medium of photography. They argued that the one thing photography could do that painting could not was render sharp, 'truthful' detail. To them, Cameron perverted the medium by disregarding this advantage. *The Photographic News* took this position in an early review:

> …as one of the special charms of photography consists in its completeness, details, and finish, we can scarcely commend works in which the aim appears to have been to avoid these qualities…whilst we condemn excessive sharpness we desire to see modelling and form, and not the confused image from considerable moving of the sitter, and complete absence of definition.[141]

Cameron's strongest critics were galled not just by her rejection of photographic convention, but also by the praise her photographs attracted in non-photographic periodicals. The Photographic Society exhibition committee may have had Thackeray's *Pall Mall Gazette* review in mind when it wrote a withering assessment that was reprinted in *The British Journal of Photography*:

> Admiring the enthusiasm of Mrs. Cameron, the Committee much regret that they cannot concur with the lavish praise which has been bestowed upon her productions in the non-photographic press, feeling convinced that she will herself adopt an entirely

different mode of representing her poetic ideas when she has made herself acquainted with the capabilities of the art – no sacrifices of pictorial beautify [*sic*] being demanded by nice attention to skilful manipulation and care in the selection of properly-adjusted optical instruments.[142]

Dismissing her as a novice, the committee seemed confident that once Cameron learned to use her camera correctly she would realise that beauty could in fact be rendered in sharp focus. A review published in the same journal shortly after conceded that Cameron arranged her photographs 'very artistically, very gracefully indeed' but objected to her 'slovenliness of manipulation', declaring: 'It would have been well had the fair artist paid some attention to the mechanical portion of our art-science.' The review even suggested that Cameron abandon the camera altogether and hire another photographer to realise her ideas. It stated that 'it is a subject of regret that this lady does not secure the services of an efficient operator to enable her productions to be given to the public in a more presentable form'.[143]

Her 'slovenliness of manipulation' referred not only to her supposedly incompetent handling of the camera, but also to her carelessness during other steps of the photographic process, which caused various blemishes on her prints. It is these streaks, swirls, fingerprints and other marks that many critics today interpret as satisfying signs of Cameron's process, and this aspect of her work is now widely appreciated.[144] But in her own time it generally was not.

This type of criticism had begun almost as soon as Cameron started exhibiting her work. An 1865 review enumerated the 'defects' in Cameron's photograph in evocative detail:

> A piece of collodion torn off the shoulder of *Agnes*…a broad fringe of stain three inches in length over the arm of *James Spedding*; brilliant comets flashing across *Alfred Tennyson*; tears chasing each other not only down the cheeks, but the brows, the arms, the noses, and the backgrounds of many of her best-arranged subjects.[145]

The review may have been referring to one of Cameron's earliest portraits of Tennyson, which was among the works she donated or sold to the South Kensington Museum in 1865 (p. 55). The white specks on his right temple would have been caused by dust on the plate. Flaws such as torn collodion, which prints as a black patch, are apparent in other works the Museum acquired directly from Cameron, including *Il Penseroso* and *Grace thro' Love* (pp. 125 and 134). The 'tears' the critic describes, which visibly streak two works the museum acquired later, were most likely the result of an uneven application of either developer or varnish (pp. 65 and 136). Stains and swirls feature in other works that came directly from Cameron – and therefore met with the approval of both photographer and Museum – such as *Iolande and Floss* and *The Double Star* (pp. 126–127).

The photographic flaws in both pictures enhance their dreamy, ethereal qualities. In *Iolande and Floss*, the photographic swirls merge with the drapery of the two women posing as novice nuns in love with the same nobleman in Henry Taylor's play *St Clement's Eve* (1862). In *The Double Star*, the streaks, swirls and bubbles give the print a watery effect, and the two embracing sisters appear to be floating.

A few of Cameron's contemporaries were more accepting, if not quite appreciative, of these irregularities. An 1868 review in the *Pall Mall Gazette* noted that there are 'imperfections here and there... But the imperfections are generous and undisguised, and the very inequalities seem to point out at times the special beauties of her workmanship'.[146] The Jury of the Dublin Exhibition of 1865 also declared Cameron's pictures 'the works of a true artist' while acknowledging their technical flaws. They warned against the tendency to dismiss them outright, recommending they be viewed repeatedly for a true understanding of their values:

> There is no experienced judge who would not prefer these pro-
> ductions, with their manifest imperfections, to many of the
> best-manipulated photographic portraits which are to be seen in the
> Exhibition...The more Mrs. Cameron's productions are examined,
> the more they are appreciated. At first sight they may be neglected
> and misunderstood, but at a second and a third visit her frames are
> those which at once attract attention.[147]

Five years later, a reviewer came to the opposite conclusion, strongly objecting to the glorification of Cameron's technique:

> Looked at *en masse* there is a sort of "glamour" about Mrs.
> Cameron's productions that is decidedly pleasing, but at a closer
> examination is not nearly so satisfactory. There is a sort of feeling
> after art – a suggestiveness; but that is all...Art is not art *because* it is
> slovenly, and a good picture is not improved by having the film torn,
> of being in some parts a mere indistinguishable smudge.[148]

It impossible to know the extent to which Cameron embraced such irregularities, which other photographers at the time would have rejected as technical flaws, or whether she merely tolerated them. She sometimes sought to improve her negatives, and did so with the same frankness with which she seemed to accept the streaks and swirls. For instance, in *La Madonna Vigilante/Watch without ceasing*, which she sold to the Museum in June 1865 (p. 134), Cameron scratched the emulsion off the upper right of the glass plate, perhaps initially in an attempt to remove a flaw. The scratching creates a partial halo around the Madonna and also blatantly introduces the presence of Cameron's hand in the picture.

Cameron also experimented with combination printing, by which multiple negatives are printed to form a single image. Gustave Le Gray pioneered the technique in France, combining different exposures of the sky and sea in his seascapes (fig. 22). In England,

Henry Peach Robinson, who learned the technique from Rejlander, excelled at combination printing and used it to construct genre scenes such as *When the Day's Work is Done*, which he composed from six separate negatives (fig. 23). Cameron's use of the technique was much less subtle. While Le Gray used the horizon to disguise the split between his two negatives and Robinson employed darkroom trickery to join his multiple negatives, Cameron simply printed two negatives side-by-side, leaving the seam between the two entirely visible. For *My Grandchild Archie son of Eugene Cameron R.A. aged 2 years & 3 months*, Cameron combined the bottom half of a negative of her sleeping grandson with the top half of a negative of Mary Hillier. The South Kensington Museum acquired the resulting print from her, along with a print of same image of the boy on his own (p. 128). Such deliberate interventions were apparently accepted by both Cameron and Henry Cole, and critics did not comment on them specifically.

Other interventions, such as the combination print *Daughters of Jerusalem* (p. 129) and the hybrid photograph-drawing in which Cameron scratched a picture into the background of a pious portrait of her niece Julia Jackson (p. 133), entered the V&A collection later. These are among the 67 photographs recently discovered to have once belonged to Cameron's friend and mentor G. F. Watts.

The photographs were donated to the Museum in 1941 but were not formally accessioned at the time. They reappeared in the Museum's crypt in the late 1960s, where a member of staff found them in a brown paper package marked '1941'. By then no record of the acquisition could be located and they were presumed to have been donated during World War II. The photographs were given museum accession numbers in 1969, 1981 and 1982 and were catalogued as either 'undocumented gift found in Museum vault' or of 'unknown provenance'.[149] They can now been identified – thanks to the recovery of the original acquisition file in the V&A Archive – as belonging to a group of photographs donated in 1941 by Mrs Margaret Southam, a great niece of Julia Margaret Cameron (see Appendix I).[150] In a letter accompanying the gift, Mrs Southam explained: 'I bought them at the sale at Limnerslease [the home of G. F. Watts] after the death of Mrs G. F. Watts, so they are apparently studies that Mrs Cameron gave to Mr Watts, & indeed one is so inscribed.'[151]

Mrs Southam's donation does include a photograph inscribed by Cameron: 'The Idylls of the Village / or The Idols of the Village / The Marys at the Well / of Fresh Water / a Pastoral Gem / for the Signor' (fig. 24). The 'Signor' was Cameron's pet name for Watts. Although the handwriting is unmistakably Cameron's, the authorship of the photograph is less certain. The sitters are two of Cameron's domestic servants (and frequent models) Mary Ryan and Mary Kellaway.

FIG. 23
Henry Peach Robinson (1830–1901)
When the Day's Work is Done, 1877
Albumen print
V&A: PH.723–1939

The Idylls of the Village
a The Idols of the Village
The Marys at the Well
of Fresh Water
A Pastoral gem
for the   (Signor)

(this is the name by which
his friends called G. F. Watts)

FIG. 24
Oscar Gustaf Rejlander (1813–75), possibly in collaboration with Julia Margaret
Cameron, and possibly printed by Julia Margaret Cameron
The Idylls of the Village or The Idols of the Village and reverse, c.1863
Albumen print
V&A: PH.261-1982

They pose by a well, play-acting at fetching water in a variation on scenes Rejlander photographed outside Cameron's house during his Isle of Wight visit of the early 1860s.[152] In this version, the building in the background is not the house, but rather appears to be the 'glazed fowl-house' that Cameron famously described transforming into her 'glass house' studio after receiving her first camera.[153] It is possible that Cameron collaborated with Rejlander in making the photograph, or that she printed it, as she is known to have done with other Rejlander negatives from this time.[154] The fact that she wrote a dedication to Watts on the print certainly suggests her involvement in its production, but a more definition attribution will require further research.

The presence in the Southam group of a previously untitled photograph, now identified as Diana (p. 141), that Watts sketched in an undated letter to Cameron, further supports the connection with Watts (fig. 25). Criticising the image, he wrote, 'I can't think you have taken a favourable view of the face of the young lady who posed for Diana'. He advised her not to 'put young limbs into such positions as call forth muscular development'.[155] She apparently made no further prints since this is the only known copy.

On another occasion, Watts wrote to Cameron:

> Please do not send me valuable mounted copies…send me any… defective unmounted impressions, I shall be able to judge just as well & shall be just as much charmed with success & shall not feel that I am taking money from you.[156]

Watts' request for 'defective unmounted impressions' explains why the Southam donation contains numerous examples of Cameron at her most experimental: figures stand out starkly against black backgrounds caused by missing collodion, faces swim in swirling chemical mists, or are framed by the lines of a cracked negative (pp. 135–139). Many are unique, which suggests that Cameron was not fully satisfied with them. Some may seem 'defective' but others – at least to contemporary eyes – are enhanced by their flaws, which show evidence of the artist's touch and experimentation. A photograph in the National Media Museum inscribed by Cameron 'Damaged copy – for the Signor' confirms that she heeded his desire for imperfect prints.[157]

In another letter, however, Watts urged Cameron to be more careful, especially if she hoped to sell her photographs:

> …for the interest of Art & also because I know you must turn your labour & expense into some pecuniary advantage I criticise & I am sure that you should now turn all your attention to the object of pro-ducing pictures free from those defects which are purely the result of careless, or imperfect manipulation, it is most especially with reference to the sale of your Photographs that this is so important. Artists & very great lovers of the highest qualities of Art may not &

perhaps do not care. Though the greatest art is ever the most perfect throughout, but the public will not care for any thing [*sic*] that exhibits the sort of imperfection it can understand at a glance.[158]

Watts' artistic and practical advice effectively amounted to a series of guidelines on how to be a professional artist, a path that Cameron's letters to Cole show her attempting to forge.

Viewed alongside prints the South Kensington Museum acquired from Cameron, the photographs she sent to Watts reveal details of her process. For example, two variations on *Paul and Virginia* (p. 130) that she sent to Watts show her resolving the arrangement of figures, costume and background into the final version (p. 131), which the Museum acquired in September 1865. The scene is from Jacques Henri Bernardin de Saint Pierre's tragic romance *Paul et Virginie* (1787), a novel that tells of the ill-fated love of two children (here played by Freddy Gould and Elizabeth Keown) living on Mauritius. Cameron chose to depict the passage in which the two are caught in a storm. In the story they shelter under Virginie's overskirt, but here they huddle under an umbrella. Between the first and second versions, Cameron reversed the position of the boy and girl and changed their drapery. She also extended the dark backdrop, but included the assistant's hand holding it up (p. 130). Cameron made multiple prints of the final version, so therefore seems to have been satisfied with it. Yet she still found fault with Paul's feet, and scratched into the negative to make them appear slimmer (p. 131).

The photographs that came from Watts' collection contribute to our understanding of Cameron's working process and the photographs that did meet her standards. The discovery of the provenance casts new light on dozens of the photographs in the V&A collection, which were previously indistinguishable from the rest of her œuvre and would therefore have been interpreted by anyone viewing the V&A collection as examples of Cameron's apparently low standards. Now these prints can be distinguished from those Cameron implicitly approved by offer to the Museum. They can instead be understood as unfinished sketches that she sent to Watts for comment as part of her process. The very 'defectiveness' of these prints shows Cameron to be a more discerning artist than assumed by critics both in her own time and after.

Cameron also shared her technical concerns with Henry Cole. In a letter of 12 June 1869 she complained to him about the problem of a 'honey comb crack' covering the surface of her negatives, which even the members of the Photographic Society had been unable to resolve. She wrote:

> 45 of my most precious negatives this year have perished thro
> the fault of Collodion or Varnish supplied: both or either destroy
> the film that holds the picture – you will see in the Dream the

commencement of this cruel calamity – also in the Guardian Angel – which has over taken 45 of my Gems – a honey comb crack extending over the picture appearing at any moment & beyond any power to arrest[159]

The network of cracks is apparent on the prints of *The Guardian Angel* (p. 142) and *The Dream* (p. 143) that Cameron enclosed in the letter, both of which Alan Cole donated to the Museum in 1913. The inspiration for *The Dream* was John Milton's poem, *On his deceased Wife* (c. 1658), which tells of a fleeting vision of his beloved returning to life in a dream. Cameron included G. F. Watts' assessment, 'quite divine', on the mount of the print she sent to Cole. Although she was distraught by the cracking that befell the surface of the negative, she seemed not to be bothered by the two smudged fingerprints in the lower right, which form a kind of inadvertent signature. Cameron blamed her 'fatally perishable' photographic chemicals for the cracks, while members of the Photographic Society suspected the damp climate of the Isle of Wight.[160] Today's theory is that failure to sufficiently wash the negatives after fixing them caused the problem.[161]

Two other photographs accompanied the letter: a portrait of Tennyson (p. 106) – 'my last portrait of Alfred Tennyson (not yet published) which I think you will agree with me in feeling is a National Treasure of immense value'[162] – and a portrait of Austen Henry Layard, a founder of the Arundel Society (p. 109). By sending two of her latest achievements and two of her 'gems' that had been damaged by cracks, Cameron was illustrating the urgency of printing her best pictures as soon as possible. She explained her strategy to Cole, and asked for his help with her reproductions:

> I see two grand things to remember now First to print as actively as I can whilst my precious negative is yet good Secondly to try to get the Portraits I have taken of our greatest men engraved
> Mr. Layard promised enthusiastically to help on my cause & my friends in Photography Think with a kind generous head, what you can do for me – & will you? Are there no Schools of art for which you can now send me orders – Is there no corner of the S.[outh] K[ensington] Museum where you can install me.[163]

Cameron did not commission engravings after her photographs, but instead had carbon prints made by the Autotype Company of some of the pictures she considered her most important and most valuable, including her portrait of Darwin, which she had taken during his stay in Freshwater in 1868 (p. 108). The letter demonstrates, however, Cameron's struggle to improve in the face of technical challenges as well as her continued concern about earning money from her photographs.

My Latest and I Think Almost My Best Photographs

> I have taken great pains to have my latest and I think almost my best photographs ready and framed for the Vienna exhibition.
>
> Julia Margaret Cameron to Henry Cole, 24 December 1872[164]

The last of the letters from Julia Margaret Cameron to Henry Cole preserved at the V&A is dated Christmas Eve 1872.[165] Cameron's photographs by then had been in the collection of the South Kensington Museum for over eight years, and she had been exhibiting her work in London and abroad for just as long. The letter concerns the practicalities of submitting her photographs to the 1873 Universal Exhibition in Vienna, the British contribution to which was organised by Sir Philip Cunliffe-Owen of the South Kensington Museum.[166] It is short, perhaps because Cameron was recovering from a five-week illness. But its brevity also suggests a confidence that renders extraneous language unnecessary. As Cameron wrote in *Annals of My Glass House* two years later:

> 'Mrs. Cameron's photography', now ten years old, has passed the age of lisping and stammering and may speak for itself, having travelled over Europe, America and Australia, and met with a welcome which has given it confidence and power.[167]

In 1875, the year after she wrote her account of her photographic career, Cameron was 60, her husband was 80. Four of their sons were living in Ceylon, three of them running the family coffee plantations and one a civil servant, and the Camerons decided to leave England and join them. Their luggage included two coffins in anticipation of their deaths.[168] Once in Ceylon, Cameron's photographic production slowed considerably. The relatively few photographs she made there are mainly studies of domestic and plantation workers.[169] The only photograph by Cameron from Ceylon in the V&A collection is a portrait taken in 1877 of the botanical painter Marianne North, the sole European to sit for Cameron there (p. 114). Julia Margaret Cameron died in 1879, followed by her husband a year later.

Cameron's presence in the V&A did not, of course, end with her letter of 1872. In the decades since, the Museum's collection of her photographs has expanded, and her works have been displayed on its walls, researched in its Prints and Drawings Study Room, and lent to institutions around the world. Cameron is present not only in her photographs and letters to Cole, but in the registers and other archival papers that provide clues to her relationship with the Museum. As the exploration of this material shows, the story of Julia Margaret Cameron at the V&A is the story of the development of an artist.

Notes

1. Heinz Archive and Library, National Portrait Gallery, London. Reproduced in Ford 1975, p. 141.

2. For further details of Cameron's biography, see Olsen 2003; Ford 2003; and Colin Ford, 'Geniuses, Poets, and Painters: The World of Julia Margaret Cameron' in Cox and Ford 2003, pp. 11–39.

3. I am indebted to Erika Lederman for the many hours she spent enthusiastically locating and meticulously collating that material, as well as to James Sutton and Christopher Marsden of the V&A Archive for helping us navigate and access it.

4. National Art Library, Victoria and Albert Museum, MSL/1934/3537/8/2/1/1.

5. Henry Cole diary, 19 May 1865, National Art Library, Victoria and Albert Museum, MSL/1934/4142.

6. Watts was jokingly said to have come to stay for three days but ending up staying for 30 years. Ford in Cox and Ford 2003, p. 18.

7. For further details on Little Holland House, see Olsen 2003, pp. 77–107.

8. The diary entry also shows the intersection of Cole's social and professional activities. It continues: 'Mr Prinsep assisting, & the Irish girls. Saw Watts who promised to produce his design by 1st June.'

9. Cameron inscribed the print of this photograph in the Overstone album (J. Paul Getty Museum) 'Little Holland House Lawn, May 1865'.

10. A later critic, describing Cameron's use of long exposures, claimed that she sometimes 'waved an umbrella in front of the lens during exposure, shading off the lights from various parts, and necessarily still more protracting the exposure.' 'Long Exposures', *The Photographic News* (19 December 1873), p. 606.

11. The original manuscript is in the Royal Photographic Society Collection at the National Media Museum, Bradford. It has been reprinted in various publications. I will refer to the annotated version in Hamilton 1996, pp. 11–16. For a full list of reprints, see Julian Cox, '"To … startle the eyes with wonder & delight": The Photographs of Julia Margaret Cameron' in Cox and Ford 2003, p. 75, note 52.

12. Cameron, *Annals* in Hamilton 1996, p. 11. Cameron wrote to Herschel on 26 February 1864: 'At the beginning of this year I first took up Photography & my kind and loving son Charles Norman gave me a camera & I set to work alone & unassisted to see what I could do.' Royal Society, quoted by Cox in Cox and Ford 2003, p. 45. Although the letter seems to contradict both the date of the gift and its donor, it is possible that she did receive the camera in December 1863, but only began using it January 1864, and that she was using her son-in-law's name as shorthand for her daughter and husband.

13. Cameron, *Annals*, in Hamilton 1996, p. 12.

14. See Joanne Lukitsh, 'Before 1864: Julia Margaret Cameron's Early Work in Photography' in Cox and Ford 2003, pp. 95–105, and Mulligan et al. 1994.

15. Her first camera was equipped with a French-made Jamin lens with a fixed aperture of f3.6 and a focal length of about 12 in. The second camera had a Rapid Rectilinear Dallmayer lens with an aperture of f8 and a focal length of 30 in. For a thorough discussion of Cameron's process and equipment, see Wolf 1998, pp. 208–18, and Cox, in Cox and Ford 2003, pp. 47–52 and 63.

16. Cameron, *Annals*, in Hamilton 1996, p. 12.

17. Henry Herschel Hay Cameron later became a professional portrait photographer.

18. Cameron wrote to Herschel shortly after acquiring her camera: 'I have had one lesson from the great amateur Photographer Mr. Wynfield & I consult him in correspondence whenever I am in a difficultly but he has not yet seen my successes.' 26 February 1864, Royal Society, London, quoted in Olsen 2003, p. 145. Wynfield was one of the artists commissioned by the South Kensington Museum in the 1860s to paint decorative lunettes illustrating aspects of art education above the two rooms known as the National Competition Gallery. One of those rooms, now designated Gallery 100, is the present-day Photographs Gallery. Cameron's nephew, Val Prinsep, also contributed a painting to the scheme. See: vam.ac.uk/content/articles/l/lunettes/

19. *The Photographic News* (15 July 1864), p. 340.

20. Cox and Ford 2003, cat. nos 31–2, 761–90.

21. Cameron, *Annals*, in Hamilton 1996, p. 13.

22. The album is now in the collection of the J. Paul Getty Museum, Los Angeles. See Weaver 1986. Many of the photographs Cameron selected for the Overstone album were the same as the ones the South Kensington Museum acquired in June, July, and September of the same year.

23. The Watts album is in the collection of the George Eastman House, Rochester, NY. See Lukitsh 1986. For an overview of Cameron's most important albums, see Appendix C, 'Albums', in Cox and Ford 2003, pp. 502–5.

24. For more on the role of women in Cameron's photographs, see Wolf 1998 and McCauley 2011.

25. Photographs only became eligible for copyright protection with the Copyright Act of 1862. From May 1864 to October 1875, Cameron registered 508 photographs. For a list of all of the photographs Cameron registered for copyright, see Wood 1996. See also Appendix A, 'Copyright Registers', in Cox and Ford 2003, pp. 496–7.

26 Cameron was elected a member of the Photographic Society of London on 7 June 1864. *The Photographic Journal* (15 June 1864), p. 51. She remained a member until 1879, when her address was still listed as Freshwater Bay, Isle of Wight. I am grateful to Michael Pritchard for providing these details. For an extensive list of 'Selected Exhibitions', see Cox and Ford 2003, pp. 538–44.

27 *The Photographic News* (3 June 1864), p. 266.

28 The main British photographic journals by the mid-1860s were *The British Journal of Photography*; *The Photographic Journal*, which was the journal of the Photographic Society, later renamed the Royal Photographic Society; *The Photographic News*; and *Photographic Notes*.

29 *The Photographic Journal* (15 August 1865), p. 126.

30 *The British Journal of Photography* (19 May 1865), p. 267.

31 Cameron, *Annals*, in Hamilton 1996, p. 13.

32 For instance, *The British Journal of Photography* accused Cameron of 'questionable taste' for exhibiting *The Angel at the Sepulchre* (p. 96) with the words 'very beautiful / none better / G.F. Watts' inscribed on the mount. 'The Photographs at the International Exhibition', *The British Journal of Photography* (9 May 1873), p. 216. She went on to make further prints of the image with the inscription reproduced in lithograph on the mounts.

33 Julia Margaret Cameron to Henry Cole, 20 May 1865, National Art Library, Victoria and Albert Museum, MSL/1934/3537/8/2/1/1.

34 On 16 July 1864, *The Athenaeum* noted that Cameron's photographs were available from Colnaghi, p. 88. For more on Cameron's relationship with the gallery, see Cox and Ford 2003, pp. 499–500.

35 *The British Journal of Photography* (13 January 1865), p. 20.

36 See 'Selected Exhibitions', Cox and Ford 2003, p. 538.

37 *The British Journal of Photography* (13 January 1865), p. 20.

38 *The British Journal of Photography* (2 June 1865), p. 292.

39 It is the only surviving set of the complete series. It was transferred to the V&A in 2000 having been remounted separately at an earlier date.

40 Julia Margaret Cameron to Henry Cole, 20 May 1865, National Art Library, Victoria and Albert Museum, MSL/1934/3537/8/2/1/1.

41 Cox in Cox and Ford 2003, p. 77, note 105.

42 Julia Margaret Cameron to Henry Cole, 20 May 1865, National Art Library, Victoria and Albert Museum, MSL/1934/3537/8/2/1/1.

43 V&A Archive, MA/4/1, Correspondence abstracts and registers: registered papers RP/1865/12067.

44 The purchase consisted of two duplicate sets of 20 photographs each, one set of 19 (also a duplicate set, but without a copy of *Sappho*), and four Madonna groups. Cole designated one set for the Art Library, two for the Circulation Department (which sent loan exhibitions around the country) and the remaining four for Godfrey Sykes, the designer responsible for internal and external decoration of the South Kensington Museum. The library set has not been located and was noted missing as early as 1926. The remaining 39 photographs are still in the collection, comprising 19 pairs of duplicates and one unique print of *Sappho*.

45 The dates are those on which the acquisitions were recorded in the Library Receiving Room Diaries, V&A Archive, and the Photographs Acquisition Register, Word & Image Department, V&A. All but two of the further 51 acquired in July and September are still in the collection. Together with the 39 from the initial purchase, there are now 88 photographs acquired directly from the artist in the V&A.

46 The V&A now holds 252 photographs by Cameron, 46 of which are unique prints.

47 In the Library Receiving Room Diary, in which all works entering the collection of the library were recorded, prices are written alongside the photographs acquired in July and September, as for the purchase of 17 June (V&A Archive, Library Receiving Room Diary volume 5, MA/34/5). The entries for 28 and 31 July also makes reference to two invoices dated 10 August 1865, one with the same number as the invoice for the 17 June purchase, and one with a different invoice number. This further suggests that the photographs were purchased, but the invoices themselves no longer exist, so this cannot be confirmed. The entry in the Library Receiving Room Diary for 27 September 1865, however, implies that the acquisition was a gift since it includes the note: '"These photographs are presented to the Museum by Mrs Cameron as specimens of her photography." A.[lan] S. Cole.' Further clues are scattered in the correspondence abstracts, the official summaries of museum correspondence, of which the originals do not survive. Most suggestively, Cameron acknowledged payment of £9.15.0 on 19 April 1866, and £30.12.0 on 2 May 1866. (See V&A Archive, MA/4/2, Correspondence abstracts and registers: registered papers RP/1866/12415 and MA/4/3; Correspondence abstracts and registers: registered papers RP/1866/13515.) The first figure is the sum of the prices recorded for the acquisition of 27 September 1865. The second is approximately a pound more than the prices for the June and July acquisitions combined. So the total of the prices of all the works the Museum acquired is almost equal to the amount Cameron was paid. However, without the actual invoices, the evidence remains inconclusive. Should further evidence emerge in the future, it may become appropriate to change the designation of these photographs, which have been referred to as gifts of the artist since 1865, to purchases from the artist.

48 Ford 1975, p. 119.

49 These consisted of eight portraits of men (including two of Tennyson and four of Henry Taylor), four of women, one of Cameron's teenage son and five of her two-year-old grandson.

50 As Mark Haworth-Booth points out, there were many higher-profile works on display at the South Kensington Museum at the time, including the Raphael tapestry cartoons, lent by Queen Victoria. Haworth-Booth 1997, pp. 81–2. Haworth-Booth published the first account of Cameron's relationship with the South Kensington Museum, and this project builds upon his important research. See Haworth-Booth 1997, pp. 79–88.

51 V&A Archive, MA/4/2, Correspondence abstracts and registers: registered papers RP/1865/20747. The letters listed in the correspondence abstracts and registers were sent to the Museum for official business and were not kept. The letters from Cameron to Henry Cole preserved in the National Art Library were personal letters to Cole and were not registered.

52 Letter from Miss Kate Perry to Mr [William] Brookfield, 33 Hans Place, 3rd Nov, 1865, in Brookfield 1905, p. 515. Cameron's only daughter, Julia Norman, would die in childbirth in 1873. In the same letter Perry relates an anecdote in which Cameron tried to re-employ her daughter's nurse by offering photographs to the nurse's new employers. As Victoria Olsen points out, neither the name nor age of the grandchild Perry mentioned was correct; Cameron's eldest grandchild was Charlotte Mary Norman, aged 5 in November 1865. Olsen 2003, p. 295, note 88. The V&A did not acquire a portrait of her until 1941 (p. 138).

53 Cameron had taken in Annie and Minnie when their father died suddenly on Christmas Eve 1863, around the same time she received her first camera. See Olsen 2003, pp. 144–5.

54 V&A Archive, MA/4/11, Correspondence abstracts and registers: registered papers RP/1875/1123. See [Anne Isabella Thackeray], 'A Book of Photographs', *Pall Mall Gazette* (10 April 1865), p. 550. Thackeray later reprinted the essay in Thackeray 1874.

55 Undated letter from G. F. Watts to Julia Margaret Cameron, Heinz Archive and Library, National Portrait Gallery, NPG P215 (1a/1b/1c).

56 On another photograph of her grandson from the same sitting Cameron wrote that the boy was 'Asleep in my dining room Freshwater Bay Isle of Wight', Cox and Ford 2003, cat. no. 149.

57 Mike Weaver has extensively researched the Christian symbolism in Cameron's photographs and in particular demonstrated the influence on Cameron of the art historian Anna Jameson, whose books included *The Poetry of Sacred and Legendary Art* (1848) and *Legends of the Madonna* (1852). See Weaver 1984 and 1986.

58 See Weaver 1984, especially p. 38.

59 Ford, in Cox and Ford 2003, p. 28. The first photographs of the Sistine Chapel, made from a scaffold, were published by Adolphe Braun et Cie. in 1869, so in 1864 Cameron would have seen prints, rather than photographs of it. See Hamber 2008, p. 1106.

60 The same prop stands in for a lyre in *Sappho* (p. 74).

61 There may have been a practical element to this as well, since, despite her forceful personality, Cameron may have found it easier to make demands of her female models, many of whom were either children or domestic staff.

62 *The Photographic Journal* (15 August 1865), p. 126.

63 Anne Thackeray noted: 'Photographers will appreciate the difficulties overcome in..."The wise and the foolish Virgins;" but it does not require any knowledge of the art to do justice to the noble and honest and beautiful effects which are here brought before us.' 'A Book of Photographs', *Pall Mall Gazette* (10 April 1865), p. 550.

64 *The British Journal of Photography* (19 May 1865), p. 267.

65 A.H. Wall, 'Practical Art Hints: A Critical Review of Artistic Progress in the Domain of Photographic Portraiture', *The British Journal of Photography* (3 November, 1865), p. 558.

66 [Anne Isabella Thackeray], 'A Book of Photographs', *Pall Mall Gazette* (10 April 1865), pp. 550–1.

67 *The Illustrated London News* quoted in 'The Exhibition of the Photographic Society', *The Photographic Journal* (15 July 1865), p. 117.

68 See Anne McCauley, 'Invading Industry: The South Kensington Museum and the Entry of Photographs into Public Museums and Libraries in the Nineteenth Century', in Haworth-Booth and McCauley 1998, pp. 33–41. McCauley notes that British art educators were quicker than their French counterparts to accept the use of photographs as study material. However she also points out that almost all the photographs collected by the South Kensington Museum for that purpose were of architecture, landscape and works of art, and not of the human figure.

69 *Index to the Collection of Photographs in the National Art Library of the South Kensington Museum* (London 1868).

70 Letter to Jane Senior, 1865, quoted by Cox, in Cox and Ford 2003, p. 76, note 83.

71 Coventry Patmore, 'Mrs Cameron's photographs', *Macmillan's Magazine* (January 1866), no. xiii, p. 231.

72 *The British Journal of Photography* (16 May 1866), p. 77.

73 *The American Journal of Photography* (15 March 1866), p. 411.

74 *The British Journal of Photography* (16 May 1866), p. 78.

75 National Art Library, Victoria and Albert Museum, MSL/1934/3537/8/2/1/2.

76 It has previously been asserted that Cameron began working with the larger camera in 1866 (see Cox, in Cox and Ford 2003, p. 63 and Wolf 1998, p. 215), but she first used the larger size for some of the photographs she took of her grandson in August 1865 (pp. 69 and 128) . Also, at least four of the photographs (*Sappho* (p. 91), *Friar Lawrence and Juliet* and *King Ahasuerus and Queen Esther* (p. 100), and *Prospero and Miranda* (V&A Museum no. 29–1939)) that she registered for copyright on 11 November 1865 were made with a larger negative. See Wood 1996, p. 8.

77 Cameron also wrote to Sir John Herschel on 18 February 1866: 'I have just been *engaged* in that which Mr. Watts has been urging me to do. A Series of Life sized heads – they are not only *from* the Life, but *to the* Life, and startle the eye with wonder and delight. I hope they will astonish the Public.' Quoted in Cox in Cox and Ford 2003 p. 65.

78 Cameron had been nursing her friend Philip Worsley on his deathbed.

79 Cameron's audience was expanding beyond Britain, and her first exhibition abroad was the Berlin International Photographic Exhibition, May–June 1865. Cox and Ford 2003, p. 538. She later exhibited in Dublin, Paris, Vienna, Sydney and Philadelphia.

80 C. Thurston Thompson, Esq., 'Official Reports of the French Exhibition', *The Photographic Journal* (16 October 1867), p. 122.

81 Julia Margaret Cameron to Sir John Herschel, 31 December 1864, Heinz Archive and Library, National Portrait Gallery, London. Reproduced in Ford 1975, pp. 141.

82 Cameron registered the first *Sappho* for copyright on 19 May 1865, and the second on 11 November 1865. See Wood 1996, pp. 7 and 9.

83 The list, annotated by Cameron, is in the collection of the National Media Museum, Bradford, and is reproduced in Wolf 1998, pp. 210–11.

84 Cameron labelled another copy of the same image *Alice No. 6*. See Cox and Ford 2003, cat. no. 877.

85 V&A Archive, MA/4/2, Correspondence abstracts and registers: registered papers RP/1866/6407 and RP/1866/11535.

86 These include *Beatrice, Christabel, Sappho, Adriana, Head of St John* and *Alice* (pp. 89–92 and 94).

87 Cameron mentions Alan Cole in four of the five letters to his father in the National Art Library. Alan Summerly Cole (1846–1934) began working at the South Kensington Museum as a Clerk in 1863, and retired in 1908 as Assistant Secretary of the Board of Education, South Kensington. I am grateful to James Sutton of the V&A Archive for providing this information.

88 The Cole family likely possessed even more photographs by Cameron. In a postscript to the 1866 letter, Cameron mentions 'the set of prints frm [*sic*] my former photos that I reserved for your Wife', and in the 1868 letter she tells Cole, 'I hope Alan gave you the brown copy of your daughter Isabella's picture'.

89 *The Photographic News* (15 June 1866), p. 279.

90 *The British Journal of Photography* (15 June 1866), p. 285.

91 See Jack 2004.

92 Cox and Ford 2003, cat. nos 406–7. Number nine of the 12 'Series of Life-sized heads of fancy Subjects' in the 1868 German Gallery catalogue is 'Beatrice, eyes down' and number ten is 'Beatrice, eyes open'. See Wolf 1998, pp. 210–11.

93 See Wolf 1998, pp. 58–60.

94 Hope Kingsley also draws this conclusion, but proposes a different print as the source image, in Kingsley 2012, p. 13. According to Colin Ford, Tennyson's home was decorated with numerous reproductions of classical sculpture and Old Master paintings, including Reni's *Beatrice Cenci* and Michelangelo's Sistine Chapel frescoes. Ford, in Cox and Ford 2003, p. 28.

95 The Duchess of Abrantes, *Lives and Portraits of Celebrated Women of all Countries* (London 1834), prospectus (unpaginated).

96 'The International Exhibition', *The British Journal of Photography* (25 October 1872), p. 506.

97 *The Photographic News* (15 June 1866), p. 279.

98 *Art Pictorial and Industrial* (1870), I.6, p. 125.

99 *The Morning Post* (27 January 1868), p. 2.

100 This point of view persisted for most of the 20th century. In his influential monograph on Cameron (first published in 1948), Helmut Gernsheim wrote: 'If Mrs Cameron's illustrations appear to us affected, ludicrous and amateurish, and must on the whole be condemned as failures from an aesthetic standpoint, how masterly, in contrast, are her straightforward, truthful portraits, which are entirely free from sentiment and compensate for the errors of taste in her studies.' Gernsheim 1975, p. 62. For a concise overview of critical responses to Cameron's staged photographs, see Colin Ford, 'Illustrations', in Cox and Ford 2003, pp. 433–4. Today, for viewers accustomed to postmodernist photographs that deliberately draw attention to their own artifice, Cameron's staged photographs are no longer so problematic. For a consideration of Cameron in the context of modern and contemporary staged photography, see Pauli 2006.

101 'Mrs. Cameron's Photographs', *Pall Mall Gazette* (29 January 1868), p. 394.

102 Coventry Patmore, 'Mrs Cameron's photographs', *Macmillan's Magazine* (January 1866), no. xiii, p. 231.

103 *The British Journal of Photography* (25 July 1873), p. 351.

104 See Debra N. Mancoff, 'Legend "From Life": Cameron's Illustrations to Tennyson's "Idylls of the King"' in Wolf 1988, pp. 87–106; Ford, 'Idylls' in Cox and Ford 2003, pp. 467–8 and Carol Armstrong, 'Photographing Literature: Julia Margaret Cameron's Excerpts from Tennyson' in Armstrong 1998, pp. 361–421.

105 [Agnes Mangles], 'A Reminiscence of Mrs. Cameron by a Lady Amateur', *The Photographic News* (1 January 1886), p. 3.

106 For further discussion of the relationship between Victorian staged photographs and tableaux vivants, see Marta Weiss, 'Staged Photography in the Victorian Album', in Pauli 2006, pp. 81–99.

107 National Art Library, Victoria and Albert Museum, MSL/1934/3537/8/2/1/3.

108 Cameron, *Annals*, in Hamilton 1996, p. 15.

109 *The Photographic Journal* (15 February 1865), p. 196.

110 Cameron, *Annals*, in Hamilton 1996, p. 15.

111 *The Standard* (28 January 1868), p. 6.

112 No museum records of Cameron's residency have been located. The mention of the use of two rooms occurs in a personal letter to Cole, not in one that was recorded in the Museum's correspondence abstracts or minutes. In 1868 photographic operations at the South Kensington Museum were in flux. Charles Thurston Thompson, the Museum's first official photographer, died 20 January 1868. His sister, Isabel Cowper, seems to have taken over soon after, first producing prints from Thompson's negatives and then beginning to make her own. Her name first appears in the Museum's photographs' registers on 18 March 1868, around the same time that Cameron set up her studio at the Museum. While the two women must have interacted, no record of contact between them has been discovered yet. See Erika Lederman, 'Isabel A. Cowper – First Female Official Photographer of the First Museum Photographic Service?' (2013). V&A blog: vam.ac.uk/blog/factory-presents/international-womens-day-historic-women-va.

113 Julia Margaret Cameron to Henry Cole, 7 April 1868, National Art Library, Victoria and Albert Museum, MSL/1934/3537/8/2/1/3.

114 See Cox and Ford 2003, cat. nos 362–4 and 476–82.

115 See Cox and Ford 2003, cat. no. 671.

116 Cameron also wrote to Cole the following year: '[E]ven now after five years of toil ardent patient persisting toil I have not yet by one hundred pounds recovered the money I have spent'. Julia Margaret Cameron to Henry Cole, 12 June 1869, National Art Library, Victoria and Albert Museum, MSL/1934/3537/8/2/1/4. As Sylvia Wolf points out, it was highly unconventional at the time for a woman to write so openly about financial matters. Wolf 1998, p. 213.

117 Typescript of the diaries of Sir Henry Cole, National Art Library, V&A, Cole Collection, pressmark 55.cc. Cole also wrote on 17 March 1868, 'Museum Mrs. Cameron photographing.'

118 This portrait was previously thought to have been made at Little Holland House in May 1865, but its larger format (12 5/8 × 9 ½ in; about 33 × 24 cm) suggests it was made after August 1865. Given that Cole mentions being photographed by Cameron only twice, the later date of March 1868 seems most likely.

119 The Morning Post (18 March 1868), p. 1.

120 The most expensive works, at 21 shillings, were portraits of Tennyson (autographed) and Mrs Herbert Duckworth. For a thorough analysis of Cameron's pricing, see Wolf 1998, pp. 208–18.

121 Joachim gave several concerts in London that March, and on 7 April, The Times reported that he had just given his last concert in England for the year. The Times (7 April 1868), p. 6.

122 See Cox and Ford 2003, cat. no. 227.

123 Cameron listed another one from the series, 'Capt Speedy with Child on lap full face' at £1 (or 20 shillings, the same price as a portrait of Herschel 'with genuine autograph').

124 'Mrs. Cameron's Photographs', Pall Mall Gazette (27 July 1868), p. 314.

125 James 1998, p. 520. The Illustrated London News announced: 'The Royal treasures from Abyssinia are open to inspection of the public at the South Kensington Museum, by command of her Majesty.' 'Metropolitan News', The Illustrated London News (4 July 1868), p. 3.

126 See Cox and Ford 2003, cat. no. 717.

127 See Rosen 1998, pp. 158–86.

128 Coventry Patmore, 'Mrs Cameron's photographs', Macmillan's Magazine (January 1866), no. xiii, p. 230.

129 Cameron, Annals, in Hamilton 1996, p. 12.

130 The Photographic News (3 June 1864), p. 266.

131 The Photographic Journal (15 Feb 1865), p. 196.

132 The British Journal of Photography (22 July 1864), p. 260.

133 The British Journal of Photography (25 July 1873), p. 351.

134 'The Great French Exhibition', The Times (30 September 1867), p. 8.

135 'Mrs. Cameron's Photographs', Pall Mall Gazette (29 January 1868), p. 394.

136 A.H. Wall, 'Practical Art Hints: A Critical Review of Artistic Progress in the Domain of Photographic Portraiture', The British Journal of Photography (3 November, 1865), p. 558.

137 'Mrs Cameron's Photographs', The Morning Post (23 December 1865), p. 5.

138 The Standard (9 January 1869), p. 2.

139 Cameron also printed certain negatives in reverse, which placed the emulsion side of the negative further from the paper and thereby increased the softness of the image. See Wolf 1998, pp. 70–4. For further discussion of Cameron's out-of-focus techniques see Brusius 2010 and Smith 1998, pp. 24–7 and 35–51.

140 [Anne Isabella Thackeray], 'A Book of Photographs', Pall Mall Gazette (10 April 1865), p. 550.

141 The Photographic News (15 July 1864), p. 340.

142 The British Journal of Photography (12 May 1865), p. 249.

143 'The Photographic Society's Exhibition', The British Journal of Photography (19 May 1865), p. 267.

144 See, in particular, Armstrong 1996 and Mavor 1995, especially pp. 44–64. Both authors link the tactile nature of Cameron's photographs to her maternal experience.

145 'The Photographic Society's Exhibition', The British Journal of Photography (19 May 1865), p. 267.

146 'Mrs. Cameron's Photographs', Pall Mall Gazette (29 January 1868), p. 394.

147 'Dublin Exhibition: Report of the Jury, and the List of Awards', The Photographic Journal (16 October 1865), p. 165.

148 Benjn. Wyles, 'Impressions of the Photographic Exhibition', The British Journal of Photography (9 December 1870), p. 578.

149 The photographs accessioned in 1981 were noted to have been 'found in the Crypt by Mr Peter Castle during the late 1960s in a brown paper package marked "1941"'. Photographs Acquisition Register, 1981, Word & Image Department, V&A. It is now evident that the Cameron photographs accessioned in 1969, 1981 and 1982 were from the same 1941 donation, even though the note about their discovery in the crypt appears only in the 1981 acquisition record.

150 I am grateful to Erika Lederman and James Sutton for locating the original acquisition file.

151 V&A Archive, MA/37/1/219, Library Administration File VAL (G)16/125. The Limnerslease sale was held 13–15 March 1939. The gift included the photograph by Rejlander that Cameron printed surrounded by fern leaves (p. 132), as well as three other portraits of women previously attributed to Cameron, but apparently by Rejlander and possibly printed by Cameron (Museum numbers PH.358-1981, PH.259-1982 and PH.260-1982). Two of these (PH.259-1982 and PH.358-1981, printed in reverse) are included in the album Cameron inscribed

'photographs of my own printing' for her sister Virginia Somers-Cocks in December 1863.

152 Two photographs from the same sitting are in the 'Mia' album, which Cameron gave to her sister, Maria Jackson. See Ovenden 1975, plates 29 and 88 and Mulligan et al. 1994 pp. 47 and 60.

153 Cameron, *Annals*, in Hamilton 1996, p. 12.

154 See Lukitsh in Cox and Ford 2003, pp. 95–105.

155 Undated letter from G.F. Watts to Julia Margaret Cameron, Heinz Archive and Library, National Portrait Gallery, NPG P125 (2a/2b).

156 Undated letter from G.F. Watts to Julia Margaret Cameron, Heinz Archive and Library, National Portrait Gallery, NPG P215 (1a/1b/1c).

157 Cox and Ford 2003, cat. no. 874.

158 Undated letter from G.F. Watts to Julia Margaret Cameron, Heinz Archive and Library, National Portrait Gallery, NPG P125 (3a/3b/3c/3d).

159 Julia Margaret Cameron to Henry Cole, 12 June 1869, National Art Library, Victoria and Albert Museum, MSL/1934/3537/8/2/1/4.

160 Cameron brought her problem to the Photographic Society in May 1869. See 'Cracking of Collodion Negatives', *The British Journal of Photography* (14 May 1869), p. 229 and 'London Photographic Society', *The British Journal of Photography* (14 May 1869), p. 234. The following month, an item in the same journal noted: 'when Mrs. Cameron made her plaint respecting the cracking of her negatives, the members came forward in a gallant manner to rescue their self-possessed sister'. 'A Peripatetic Photographer', 'Notes on Passing Events', *The British Journal of Photography* (4 June 1869), p. 268.

161 See Cox in Cox and Ford 2003, p. 48 and p. 74, note 48.

162 She also enclosed a copy for Annie and Minnie Thackeray, and asked Cole to pass it on to them.

163 Julia Margaret Cameron to Henry Cole, 12 June 1869, National Art Library, Victoria and Albert Museum, MSL/1934/3537/8/2/1/4.

164 Julia Margaret Cameron to Henry Cole, 24 December 1872, National Art Library, Victoria and Albert Museum, MSL/1934/3537/8/2/1/5.

165 'Dear Mr Cole' is now 'My Dear Sir Henry Cole', however Cole was not knighted until 1875.

166 Cameron was awarded a medal for 'good taste'. 'Photographic Awards at the Vienna Exhibition', *The Photographic News* (29 August 1873), p. 415. Cunliffe-Owen succeeded Cole as director of the Museum in 1874.

167 Cameron, *Annals*, in Hamilton 1996, p. 11.

168 Olsen 2003, p. 244.

169 See Cox and Ford 2003, pp. 483–95.

Plates

Unless otherwise noted, all photographs are by Julia Margaret Cameron
and are albumen prints from wet collodion negatives.
Titles in italics are those given by Cameron.

From First Success
to the South Kensington Museum

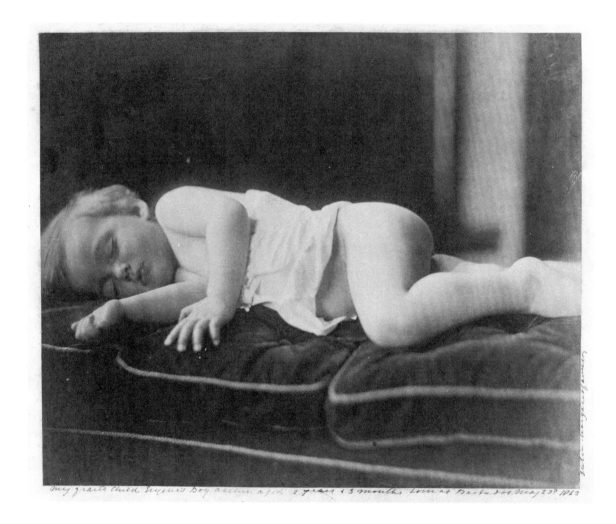

Alfred Tennyson
1864
V&A: 45132

Henry Taylor
1864
V&A: 45135

Lord Elcho
1865
V&A: 45138

Sir Coutts Lindsay
1865
V&A: 45131

The Shadow of the Cross
1865

Devotion
1865

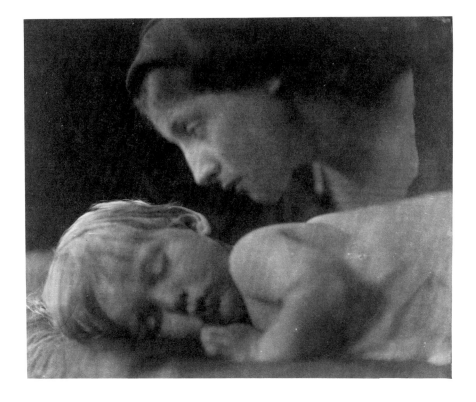

Fruits of the Spirit
1864

The five Wise Virgins
1864
V&A: 44778

The five foolish Virgins
1864
V&A: 44779

Spring
1865
V&A: 44776

The Anniversary
1865
V&A: 44963

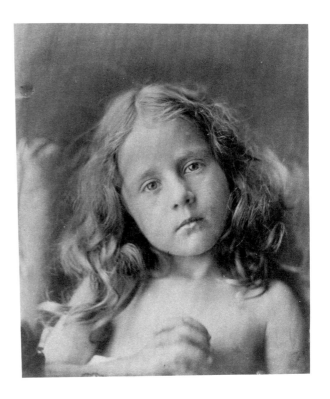

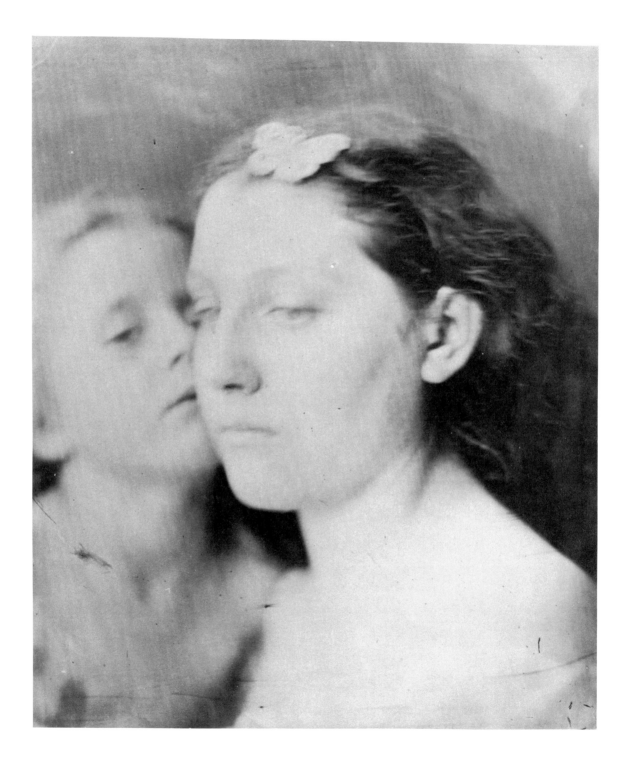

Electrify and Startle

Adriana
1866
V&A: 943–1913

Head of St. John
1866
V&A: 938–1913

Unknown girl
1865–6
V&A: E.2743–1990

The Angel at the Sepulchre
1869–70
V&A: 936–1913

Friar Laurence and Juliet
1865
V&A: 941–1913

King Ahasuerus & Queen Esther in Apocrypha
1865
V&A: 942–1913

Fortune as well as Fame

Henry John Stedman Cotton
1867
V&A: E.2754–1990

Henry Taylor
1867
V&A: 1142–1963

Florence Fisher
1872
V&A: 209–1969

Dèjatch Alámayou
1868
V&A: 24–1939

ILLUSTRATIONS

TO TENNYSON'S

IDYLLS OF THE KING,

AND OTHER POEMS.

BY

JULIA MARGARET CAMERON.

HENRY S. KING & Co.,
65, CORNHILL, AND 12, PATERNOSTER ROW, LONDON.
1875.

Merlin and Vivien

For Merlin overtalk'd and overworn,
Had yielded, told her all the charm and slept

Then in one moment, she put forth the charm
Of woven paces and of waving hands
And in the hollow oak he lay as dead,
And lost to life and use, and name and fame.

A Tennyson

The May Queen.

You must wake and call me early, call me early Mother dear;
To morrow 'll be the happiest time of all the glad New Year;
Of all the glad New Year, Mother, the maddest merriest day;
For I'm to be Queen of the May Mother, I'm to be Queen o' the May.

There's many a black black eye they say, but none so bright as mine;
There's Margaret and Mary, there's Kate and Caroline:
But none so fair as little Alice in all the land they say
So I'm to be Queen o' the May Mother, I'm to be Queen o' the May.

I sleep so sound all night, Mother, that I shall never wake,
If you do not call me loud when the day begins to break
But I must gather knots of flowers, and buds and garlands gay,
For I'm to be Queen o' the May mother, I'm to be Queen o' the May.

As I came up the valley whom think ye should I see,
But Robin leaning on the bridge beneath the hazel-tree
He thought of that sharp look Mother, I gave him yesterday—
But I'm to be Queen o' the May, mother I'm to be Queen o' the May.

He thought I was a ghost, Mother, for I was all in white,
And I ran by him without speaking, like a flash of light
They call me cruel-hearted, but I care not what they say,
For I'm to be Queen o' the May, mother, I'm to be Queen o' the May.

They say he's dying all for love but that can never be;
They say his heart is breaking mother— what is that to me?
There's many a bolder lad 'ill woo me any summer day,
And I'm to be Queen o' the May, mother, I'm to be Queen o' the May.

Little Effie shall go with me to morrow to the green,
And you'll be there too mother, to see me made the Queen;
For the Shepherd lads on every side 'ill come from far away,
And I'm to be Queen o' the May mother, I'm to be Queen o' the May.

The honey-suckle round the Rock has wov'n the wavy bowers
And by the Meadow trenches blow the faint sweet cuckoo flowers
And the wild marsh-marigold shines like fire in swamps and hollows gray;
And I'm to be Queen o' the May mother, I'm to be Queen o' the May.

The night winds come and go Mother, upon the meadow-grass,
And the happy stars above them seem to brighten as they pass;
There will not be a drop of rain the whole of the live long day,
And I'm to be Queen o' the May mother, I'm to be Queen o' the May.

All the valley Mother 'll be fresh and green and still,
And the cowslip and the crowfoot are over all the hill,
And the rivulet in the flowery dale 'ill merrily glance and play,
For I'm to be Queen o' the May, Mother, I'm to be Queen o' the May
So you must wake and call me early, call me early, Mother dear,
To morrow 'ill be the happiest time of all the glad new year;
To morrow 'ill be of all the year the maddest merriest day,
For I'm to be Queen o' the May Mother, I'm to be Queen o' the May.

The Passing of Arthur

Then saw they how there hove a dusky barge,
Dark as a funeral scarf from stem to stern,
Beneath them; and descending they were ware
That all the decks were dense with stately forms,
Black-stoled, black-hooded, like a dream — by these
Three Queens with crowns of gold: and from them rose
A cry that shiver'd to the tingling stars,
And, as it were one voice, an agony
Of lamentation, like a wind that shrills
All night in a waste land, where no one comes,
Or hath come, since the making of the world.

Then murmur'd Arthur, 'Place me in the barge'
So to the barge they came. There those three Queens
Put forth their hands, and took the King, and wept.
But she, that rose the tallest of them all
And fairest, laid his head upon her lap,
And loosed the shatter'd casque, and chafed his hands,
And call'd him by his name, complaining loud.

. . . .
. . . .

So like a shatter'd column lay the King.

A Tennyson

Her Mistakes Were Her Successes

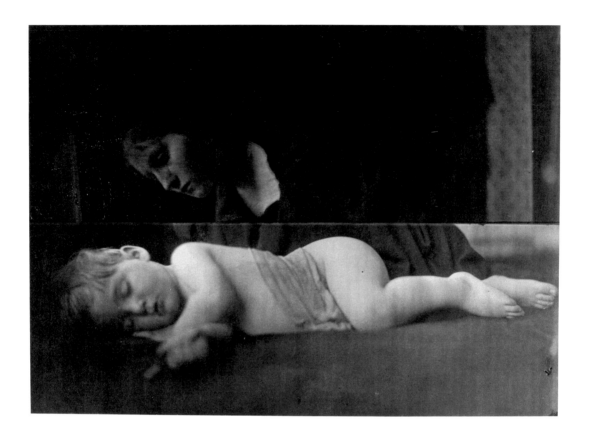

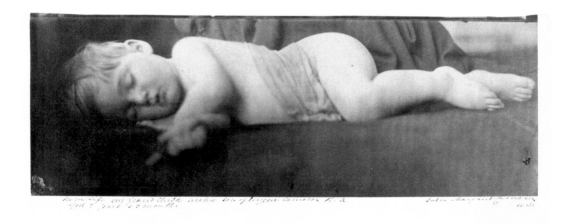

Paul and Virginia
1864
V&A: 218–1969

Paul and Virginia
1864
V&A: PH.247–1982

Oscar Gustaf Rejlander (1813–75), printed by Julia Margaret Cameron
Kate Dore
c.1862

La Madonna Vigilante / Watch without ceasing
1864
V&A: 44748

Grace thro' Love
1865
V&A: 44750

Madonna and Child
1864–5
V&A: PH.338–1981

Mary Hillier
1864–6
V&A: PH.346–1981

Group (Alice Keown, Elizabeth Keown?,
Mary Kellaway and Percy Keown)
1864
V&A: PH.332–1981

Group (Alice Du Cane and unknown woman)
1864–5
V&A: PH.353–1981

Hosanna
1865
V&A: PH.244–1982

Hosanna
1865
V&A: PH.243–1982

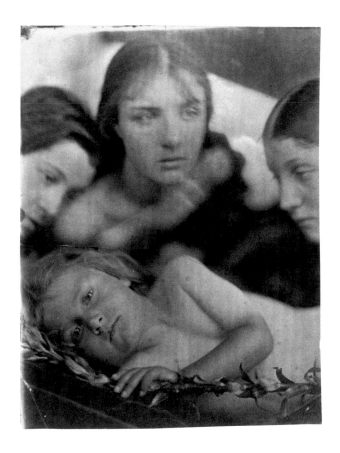

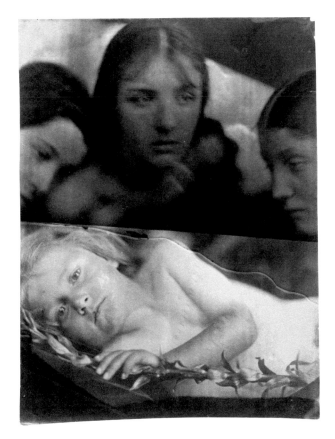

Select Bibliography

Allingham and Radford 1907

H. Allingham and D. Radford (eds), *William Allingham, A Diary* (London 1907)

Armstrong 1996

Carol Armstrong, 'Cupid's Pencil of Light: Julia Margaret Cameron and the Maternalization of Photography', *October*, no. 76 (Spring 1996), pp. 114–41

Armstrong 1998

Carol Armstrong, *Scenes in a Library: Reading the Photograph in the Book*, 1843–1875 (Cambridge, MA 1998)

Bonython 1982

Elizabeth Bonython, *King Cole: A Picture Portrait of Sir Henry Cole*, KCB 1808-1882 (London 1982)

Brookfield 1905

Charles and Frances Brookfield, *Mrs Brookfield and Her Circle*, vol. II (1848–1874) (New York 1905)

Brusius 2010

Mirjam Brusius, 'Impreciseness in Julia Margaret Cameron's Portrait Photographs', *History of Photography* (November 2010), vol. 34, no. 4, pp. 342–55

Bryant 2011

Julius Bryant, ed., *Art and Design for All: The Victoria and Albert Museum* (London 2011)

Cox 1996

Julian Cox, *Julia Margaret Cameron: Photographs from the J. Paul Getty Museum* (Los Angeles 1996)

Cox and Ford 2003

Julian Cox and Colin Ford, *Julia Margaret Cameron: the Complete Photographs* (Los Angeles 2003)

Ford 1975

Colin Ford, *The Cameron Collection: An Album of Photographs by Julia Margaret Cameron Presented to Sir John Herschel* (Wokingham 1975)

Ford 2003

Colin Ford, *Julia Margaret Cameron: a Critical Biography* (Los Angeles 2003)

Gernsheim 1975

Helmut Gernsheim, *Julia Margaret Cameron: Her Life and Photographic Work*, 2nd edition (London 1975)

Hamber 2008

Anthony Hamber, 'Photography of Paintings' in John Hannavy (ed.), *Encyclopedia of Nineteenth Century Photography* (New York 2008)

Hamilton 1996

Violet Hamilton, *Annals of My Glass House* (Claremont, CA 1996)

Haworth-Booth 1997

Mark Haworth-Booth, *Photography: An Independent Art* (London 1997)

Haworth-Booth and McCauley 1998

Mark Haworth Booth and Anne McCauley, *The Museum & the Photograph: Collecting Photography at the Victoria and Albert Museum, 1853–1900* (Williamstown, MA 1998)

Hopkinson 1986

Amanda Hopkinson, *Julia Margaret Cameron* (London 1986)

Jack 2004

Belinda Jack, *Beatrice's Spell: The Enduring Legend of Beatrice Cenci* (London 2004)

James 1998

Elizabeth James, *The Victoria and Albert Museum: A Bibliography and Exhibition Chronology, 1852–1996* (London and Chicago 1998)

Kingsley 2012

Hope Kingsley, *Seduced by Art: Photography Past and Present* (London 2012)

Lukitsh 1986

Joanne Lukitsh, *Cameron: Her Work and Career* (Rochester, NY 1986)

Lukitsh 2001

Joanne Lukitsh, *Julia Margaret Cameron* (London 2001)

McCauley 2011

Anne McCauley, 'Brides of Men and Brides of Art:

The "Woman Question" of the 1860s and the Photographs of Julia Margaret Cameron', *Études photographiques* (November 2011), no. 28, pp. 6–75

Mavor 1995

Carol Mavor, *Pleasures Taken: Performances of Sexuality and Loss in Victorian Photographs* (Durham, NC 1995)

Mulligan et al. 1994

Therese Mulligan et al., *For My Best Beloved Sister Mia* (Albuquerque, NM 1994)

Olsen 2003

Victoria Olsen, *From Life: Julia Margaret Cameron & Victorian Photography* (London 2003)

Ovenden 1975

Graham Ovenden (ed.), *A Victorian Album: Julia Margaret Cameron and Her Circle* (London 1975)

Pauli 2006

Lori Pauli (ed.), *Acting the Part: Photography as Theatre* (London 2006)

Physick 1982

John Physick, *The Victoria and Albert Museum: The History of Its Building* (London 1982)

Roberts 1992

Pam Roberts, 'Julia Margaret Cameron: A Triumph over Criticism', in *The Portrait in Photography*, Graham Clarke (ed.), (London 1992), pp. 47-70.

Rosen 1998

Jeff Rosen, 'Cameron's photographic double takes' in J. F. Codell and D. S. Macleod (eds), *Orientalism Transposed: The Impact of the Colonies on British Culture* (Aldershot 1998)

Smith 1998

Lindsay Smith, *The Politics of Focus: Women, Children and Nineteenth-Century Photography* (Manchester 1998)

Thackeray 1874

Anne Isabella Thackeray, *Toilers and Spinsters and Other Essays* (London 1874)

Thackeray Ritchie and Cameron 1893

Anne Thackeray Ritchie and H. H. Hay Cameron, *Alfred, Lord Tennyson and His Friends* (London 1893)

Waggoner 2010

Diane Waggoner, *The Pre-Raphaelite Lens: British Photography and Painting, 1848-1875* (Washington 2010)

Weaver 1984

Mike Weaver, *Julia Margaret Cameron, 1815–1879* (London 1984)

Weaver 1986

Mike Weaver, *Whisper of the Muse: The Overstone Album and Other Photographs by Julia Margaret Cameron* (Los Angeles 1986)

Wolf 1998

Sylvia Wolf, *Julia Margaret Cameron's Women* (Chicago 1998)

Wood 1996

R. Derek Wood, 'Julia Margaret Cameron's Copyrighted Photographs', unpublished booklet, London, 1996. Available at midley.co.uk/cameron/cameron.pdf

Woolf and Fry 1926

Virginia Woolf and Roger Fry, *Victorian Photographs of Famous Men and Fair Women* (London 1926)

Appendix I
Complete List of Works

This list of Cameron's works in the collection of the Victoria and Albert Museum is organised by date and source of acquisition. Titles in italics are those given by Cameron, either on the mounts of prints in the V&A, or on other prints of the same image. Inscriptions – other than Cameron's signature line – are also italicised. Unless otherwise noted, all photographs are by Julia Margaret Cameron and are albumen prints from wet collodion negatives.

Purchased from Julia Margaret Cameron 17 June 1865

La Madonna Riposata/ Resting in Hope
1865
25.5 x 21.5 cm
V&A: 44745

La Madonna della Ricordanza/Kept in the heart also known as *Peace*
1864
26.5 x 22.7 cm
V&A: 44746

La Madonna Aspettante/ Yet a little while
1865
26.7 x 20.8 cm
V&A: 44747

La Madonna Vigilante/ Watch without ceasing
1864
26 x 20.8 cm
V&A: 44748

Blessing and Blessed
1865
26 x 21.5 cm
V&A: 44749

Grace thro' Love
1865
27 x 20 cm
V&A: 44750

St. Agnes
1864
26.7 x 21.3 cm
V&A: 44751

St. Agnes
1864
26 x 21 cm
V&A: 44752

Sappho
1865
25.8 x 21.2 cm
V&A: 44753

La Madonna Esaltata/
Fervent in prayer
1864
26.7 x 21.7 cm
V&A: 44754

Iolande and Floss
c.1864
25.4 x 20.5 cm
V&A: 44755

Goodness
1864
27.5 x 22.2 cm
V&A: 44756

Spring
May 1865
25.5 x 20 cm
V&A: 44757

Spring
May 1865
26.2 x 21.5 cm
V&A: 44758

The five Wise Virgins
1864
25.5 x 21.3 cm
V&A: 44759

The five foolish Virgins
1864
26 x 20.7 cm
V&A: 44760

Yes or No?
1865
25 x 21 cm
V&A: 44761

Joy
1865
24.5 x 21.5 cm
V&A: 44762

La Madonna della
Pace/Perfect in Peace
1864
26 x 21 cm
V&A: 44763

Whisper of the Muse
1865

25.2 x 19.7 cm

V&A: 44764

*La Madonna
Riposata/
Resting in Hope*
1864

25.8 x 21.5 cm

V&A: 44765

*La Madonna della
Ricordanza/Kept in
the heart* also known
as *Peace*
1864

26 x 21.5 cm

V&A: 44766

*La Madonna
Aspettante/
Yet a little while*
1865

24.5 x 21 cm

V&A: 44767

*La Madonna Vigilante/
Watch without ceasing*
1864

25 x 21.5 cm

V&A: 44768

Blessing and Blessed
1865

25.5 x 21 cm

V&A: 44769

Grace thro' Love
1865

26 x 22 cm

V&A: 44770

St. Agnes
1864

26 x 21.6 cm

V&A: 44771

St. Agnes
1864

26 x 22 cm

V&A: 44772

*La Madonna Esaltata/
Fervent in prayer*
1864

22.5 x 21.5 cm

V&A: 44773

Iolande and Floss
c.1864

25 x 20.8 cm

V&A: 44774

Goodness
1864

25.5 x 21 cm

V&A: 44775

Spring
May 1865

26 x 21 cm

V&A: 44776

Spring
May 1865

25 x 21.5 cm

V&A: 44777

The five Wise Virgins
1864

26.5 x 21 cm

V&A: 44778

The five foolish Virgins
1864

26 x 21 cm

V&A: 44779

Yes or No?
1865

25.5 x 21 cm

V&A: 44780

Joy
1865

24.5 x 21 cm

V&A: 44781

La Madonna della Pace / Perfect in Peace
1864

24.1 x 19.9 cm

V&A: 44782

Whisper of the Muse
April 1865

26 x 21.5 cm

V&A: 44783

Given by or Purchased from Julia Margaret Cameron 28 & 31 July 1865

The Anniversary
1865

26.5 x 21 cm

V&A: 44949

The return "after three days"
1865

27.5 x 21.5 cm

V&A: 44950

A Vestal
1865

22.5 x 20 cm

V&A: 44951

Paul and Virginia
1864
26 x 20.5 cm
V&A: 44952

The red & white Roses
1865
23.5 x 21.5 cm
V&A: 44953

Lady Adelaide Talbot
May 1865
27.5 x 23.5 cm
V&A: 44954

Cupid & Psyche
1864–5
27 x 23 cm
V&A: 44955

William Michael Rossetti
May 1865
25.2 x 20.4 cm
V&A: 44956

Aged 94 Taken on the Anniversary of her 72nd Wedding day
1865
28 x 21 cm
V&A: 44957

Study of Prospero
May 1865
29.5 x 25.5 cm
V&A: 44958

The Anniversary
1865
26.5 x 21 cm
V&A: 44959

The return "after three days"
1865
28 x 23 cm
V&A: 44960

A Vestal
1864–5
26.8 x 23.7 cm
V&A: 44961

The red & white Roses
1865
26.5 x 24 cm
V&A: 44962

The Anniversary
1865
27.5 x 25.3 cm
V&A: 44963

The return
"after three days"
1865

29.5 x 24.5 cm

V&A: 44964

The Anniversary
1865

26 x 22 cm

V&A: 44965

**Given by or
Purchased from
Julia Margaret
Cameron
27 September 1865**

Sir Coutts Lindsay
1865

22.5 x 20 cm

V&A: 45131

Alfred Tennyson
1864

A. Tennyson [facsimile
signature]

27.5 x 22.8 cm

V&A: 45132

Alfred Tennyson
August 1865

A. Tennyson [facsimile
signature]

24.7 x 19.5 cm

V&A: 45133

Henry Taylor
1864

25.8 x 20.5 cm

V&A: 45134

Henry Taylor
1864

29 x 23.5 cm

V&A: 45135

Henry Taylor
1 June 1865

25.2 x 20 cm

V&A: 45136

Robert Browning
May 1865

25 x 20 cm

V&A: 45137

Lord Elcho
1865

25 x 20 cm

V&A: 45138

Lady Elcho as the
Cumaean Sybil [sic]
1865

23.5 x 20 cm

V&A: 45139

Circe
1865

Inscribed by JMC: *"Who knows not Circe/Daughter of the Sun"*

24.4 x 20.2 cm

V&A: 45140

The lily of the Valley
1864–5

25.7 x 20.5 cm

V&A: 45141

Lady Adelaide Talbot
May 1865

26 x 21 cm

V&A: 45142

Il Penseroso
1864–5

25 x 21 cm

V&A: 45143

Il Penseroso
1864–5

22.5 x 16.7 cm

V&A: 45144

Il Penseroso
1864–5

25.2 x 20.2 cm

V&A: 45145

Il Penseroso
May 1865

Inscribed by JMC: *Come pensive nun devout and pure, /Sober, stedfast and demure*

25.2 x 20.2 cm

V&A: 45146

Paul and Virginia
1864

26.6 x 21.5 cm

V&A: 45148

My grand child aged 2 years & 3 months
1865

22.3 x 27.5 cm

V&A: 45149

My grand Child Eugene's boy Archie aged 2 years & 3 months
1865

23 x 29.6 cm

V&A: 45150

My grand child aged 2 years & 3 months
1865

23.5 x 28.5 cm

V&A: 45151

My grand child aged 2 years & 3 months Archibald Cameron
1865

21 x 25.6 cm

V&A: 45152

*Henry Herschel
Hay Cameron of
Charter House*
1864

23.8 x 25.8 cm

V&A: 45153

Devotion
1865

22.8 x 27.9 cm

Inscribed by JMC: *My
grand child age 2 years &
3 months*

V&A: 45154

*St. Cecilia, after the
manner of Raphael*
1864–5

25.4 x 20 cm

V&A: 45155

*Seraphim and
Cherubim*
1864

15.5 x 8.3 cm each

V&A: 45156/1 & 45156/2

First Ideas
1865

25.5 x 20 cm

V&A: 45157

The Double Star
April 1864

25.3 x 20 cm

V&A: 45158

*My Grand Child
Archie Son of Eugene
Cameron R.A. aged
2 years & 3 months*
1865

25.5 x 36 cm

V&A: 45159

*The Shadow of
the Cross*
August 1865

27.1 x 36.5 cm

V&A: 45160

A Study
1864–5

25 x 20.5 cm

V&A: 45161

*My Grand Child
Archie Son of Eugene
Cameron R.A. aged
2 years & 3 months*
1865

12.1 x 36.8 cm

V&A: 45162

**Given by Miss
Enid DuCane
3 April 1913**

A. H. Layard M.P.
1869

Carbon print

27.5 x 22 cm

V&A: 447–1913

Mrs. Enid Layard
March 1869

Carbon print

27.8 x 20.5 cm

V&A: 448–1913

**Given by Alan S.
Cole
19 April 1913**

Henry Taylor
1865

29 x 23.8 cm

V&A: 929–1913

John Frederick
William Herschel
April 1867

*John Frederick William
Herschel* [original
signature]

34.3 x 26.6 cm

V&A: 930–1913

A. H. Layard M.P.
1869

30 x 24 cm

V&A: 931–1913

Alfred Tennyson
3 June 1869

A. Tennyson [facsimile
signature]

30.3 x 24.4 cm

V&A: 932–1913

May Day
1866

33.9 x 28.6 cm

V&A: 933–1913

Summer days
c.1866

35 x 27.2 cm

V&A: 934–1913

The Guardian Angel
1868

29.7 x 16.4 cm

V&A: 935–1913

The Angel at the
Sepulchre
1869–70

29 x 23.5 cm

V&A: 936–1913

The Dream
April 1869

quite divine/G.F. Watts
[original inscription]

30.2 x 24.3 cm

V&A: 937–1913

Head of St. John
March 1866

35.5 x 28.5 cm

V&A: 938–1913

Freddy Gould
1866
32.4 x 28.5 cm
V&A: 939–1913

Alice
1866
23.5 x 28.6 cm
V&A: 940–1913

*Friar Laurence
and Juliet*
1865
31.4 x 27.5 cm
V&A: 941–1913

*King Ahasuerus &
Queen Esther in
Apocrypha*
1865
35.6 x 29 cm
V&A: 942–1913

Adriana
May 1866
34.6 x 27 cm
V&A: 943–1913

Beatrice
March 1866
35.3 x 28.1 cm
V&A: 944–1913

Beatrice
1866
35.8 x 28.8 cm
V&A: 945–1913

Christabel
1866
33.8 x 27.7 cm
V&A: 946–1913

Sappho
1865
35.5 x 28.2 cm
V&A: 947–1913

**Presented by
the Director
1925**

Henry Taylor/A Portrait
1865, printed later
Gelatin silver print
from copy negative
25.3 x 20.2 cm
V&A: 2920–1925

Given by Miss Agnes May Ffytche 1927

Gareth and Lynette
1874

From *Illustrations to Tennyson's Idylls of the King, and Other Poems* Volume I

33.5 x 27 cm

V&A: 81–1970

Enid
1874

From *Illustrations to Tennyson's Idylls of the King, and Other Poems* Volume I

33 x 23.5 cm

V&A: 82–1970

"And Enid Sang"
September 1874

From *Illustrations to Tennyson's Idylls of the King, and Other Poems* Volume I

36 x 28 cm

V&A: 83–1970

Vivien and Merlin
1874

From *Illustrations to Tennyson's Idylls of the King, and Other Poems* Volume I

31.5 x 27.5 cm

V&A: 84–1970

Vivien and Merlin
1874

From *Illustrations to Tennyson's Idylls of the King, and Other Poems* Volume I

32 x 26.5 cm

V&A: 85–1970

Elaine "the Lily maid of Astolat"
1874

From *Illustrations to Tennyson's Idylls of the King, and Other Poems* Volume I

35 x 28 cm

V&A: 86–1970

Elaine
1874

From *Illustrations to Tennyson's Idylls of the King, and Other Poems* Volume I

32 x 25 cm

V&A: 87–1970

Sir Galahad and the Pale Nun
September 1874

From *Illustrations to Tennyson's Idylls of the King, and Other Poems* Volume I

35 x 27 cm

V&A: 88–1970

The parting of Sir Lancelot and Queen Guinevere
1874

From *Illustrations to Tennyson's Idylls of the King, and Other Poems* Volume I

35 x 28 cm

V&A: 89–1970

The little Novice with the Queen Guinevere in the Holy House at Almesbury
1874

From *Illustrations to Tennyson's Idylls of the King, and Other Poems* Volume I

35 x 26 cm

V&A: 90–1970

King Arthur
1874

From *Illustrations to Tennyson's Idylls of the King, and Other Poems* Volume I

35 x 27.5 cm

V&A: 91–1970

Freddy Gould
1866

32.4 x 28.5 cm

V&A: 1139–1933

John Frederick William
Herschel
April 1867

Carbon print

35.8 x 26.6 cm

V&A: 12–1939

T. Carlyle
1867

Carbon print

30.6 x 25.8 cm

V&A: 13–1939

Charles Darwin
1868

Carbon print

26 x 21 cm

V&A: 14–1939

*Call I Follow, I Follow.
Let Me Die*
1867

Carbon print

35 x 26.7 cm

V&A: 15–1939

Emily Peacock
1874

38.5 x 30.4 cm

V&A: 16–1939

G. F. Watts
1864

24.5 x 21 cm

V&A: 17–1939

Henry Herschel Hay Cameron
Julia Margaret Cameron
c. 1870

Inscribed by JMC: *From life Registered
Photograph Copyright Henry Herschel
Hay Cameron Freshwater*

22.9 x 19.5 cm

V&A: 18–1939

Spear or Spare
July 1868

*Báshá Félíka / Captn.
Speedy* [signature?]

31.2 x 25 cm

V&A: 19–1939

Gretchen at the Altar
1870–4

Inscribed by JMC: *See Faust*

36.7 x 27.5 cm

V&A: 20–1939

Sir Alexander Grant
1871

32.5 x 26.5 cm
V&A: 21–1939

"Three Fishers went sailing out into the West"
May 1874

36.5 x 27.5 cm
V&A: 22–1939

Zuleika / Mrs. Ewen Hay Cameron
1871

34.1 x 26 cm
V&A: 23–1939

Dèjatch Alámayou
July 1868

Dejátch Álámáyou [signature?] / [Ahmaric text] / *King Theodore's Son*

29.5 x 23.5 cm
V&A: 24–1939

Rebecca
1866, printed later

Carbon print from copy negative

36 x 29 cm
V&A: 25–1939

The Twilight hour
1874

34.5 x 27 cm
V&A: 26–1939

The Passing of King Arthur
1874

34.5 x 25.5 cm
V&A: 27–1939

Miss Louise Beatrice de Fonblanque
March 1868

Inscribed by JMC: *From Life taken at the South Kensington Museum March 1868*

32.4 x 25.4 cm
V&A: 28–1939

Prospero and Miranda
1865

33 x 27 cm
V&A: 29–1939

A Study of the Cenci
1870

33.5 x 27 cm
V&A: 30–1939

Mrs. Herbert Duckworth
1872

Carbon print from copy negative

33.5 x 24.5 cm
V&A: 31–1939

Aubry [sic] *de Vere*
1868

29.5 x 23 cm
V&A: 32–1939

Charles Hay Cameron
September 1871,
printed later

Carbon print from
copy negative

31.5 x 24.5 cm

V&A: 33–1939

Egeria
1874

38.5 x 30 cm

V&A: 34–1939

Alfred Tennyson
May 1865

From *Illustrations to
Tennyson's Idylls of the
King, and Other Poems*
Volume II

25 x 20 cm

V&A: 35–1939

The May Queen
May 1875

From *Illustrations to
Tennyson's Idylls of the
King, and Other Poems*
Volume II

34 x 25.5 cm

V&A: 36–1939

New Year's Eve
May 1875

From *Illustrations to
Tennyson's Idylls of the
King, and Other Poems*
Volume II

33.9 x 25.5 cm

V&A: 37–1939

The End
1875

From *Illustrations to
Tennyson's Idylls of the
King, and Other Poems*
Volume II

34 x 25.5 cm

V&A: 38–1939

The Princess
1875

From *Illustrations to
Tennyson's Idylls of the
King, and Other Poems*
Volume II

31.5 x 24.5 cm

V&A: 39–1939

The Princess
1875

From *Illustrations to
Tennyson's Idylls of the
King, and Other Poems*
Volume II

35 x 28 cm

V&A: 40–1939

The Princess
1875

From *Illustrations to
Tennyson's Idylls of the
King, and Other Poems*
Volume II

33 x 22.2 cm

V&A: 41–1939

Mariana
1874–5

From *Illustrations to
Tennyson's Idylls of the
King, and Other Poems*
Volume II

35 x 28 cm

V&A: 42–1939

The Beggar Maid
1875

From *Illustrations to
Tennyson's Idylls of the
King, and Other Poems*
Volume II

31.5 x 24.8 cm

V&A: 43–1939

Lancelot and Elaine
1875

From *Illustrations to
Tennyson's Idylls of the
King, and Other Poems*
Volume II

31.5 x 24.8 cm

V&A: 44–1939

Lancelot and Elaine
1875

From *Illustrations to
Tennyson's Idylls of the
King, and Other Poems*
Volume II

34 x 28.5 cm

V&A: 45–1939

The Passing of Arthur
c.1875

From *Illustrations to
Tennyson's Idylls of the
King, and Other Poems*
Volume II

34 x 27 cm

V&A: 46–1939

Maud
1875

32 x 27 cm

V&A: 47–1939

**Given by
Mrs Margaret
Southam
1941**

Henry Thoby Prinsep
1865

27 x 22 cm

V&A: 205–1969

Julia Jackson
1867

27.1 x 21.7 cm

V&A: 206–1969

May Prinsep
1864–6

27.5 x 21 cm

V&A: 207–1969

Julia Jackson
1864

24.6 x 19.2 cm

V&A: 208–1969

Florence Fisher
1872

36.5 x 28.3 cm

V&A: 209–1969

Henry Taylor
1864

24.2 x 19.2 cm

V&A: 210–1969

Henry Taylor
1864

24.3 x 19.2 cm

V&A: 211–1969

Henry Taylor
1864
24.2 x 19.3 cm
V&A: 212–1969

Julia Jackson, 1864
22.5 x 19 cm
V&A: 213–1969

Annie
January 1864
19.5 x 14.5 cm
V&A: 214–1969

Annie
January 1864
19.5 x 15.3 cm
V&A: 215–1969

The Infant Bridal
1864
24 x 21 cm
V&A: 216–1969

The Infant Bridal
1864
22.5 x 21 cm
V&A: 217–1969

Paul and Virginia
1864
24.5 x 19.8 cm
V&A: 218–1969

*My Grand Child Eugene's
Boy Archie aged 2 years
& 3 months born at
Barbados May 23rd 1863*
1865
23 x 28 cm
V&A: 219–1969

*Cherubim & Seraphim
continually dozing*
1864
23.4 x 21.6 cm
V&A: 220–1969

*La Madonna
Aspettante/
Yet a little while*
1865
7 x 5.5 cm
V&A: 221–1969

Maud by Moonlight
1864–5
24.5 x 19.5 cm
V&A: PH.331–1981

Group (Alice Keown,
Elizabeth Keown?,
Mary Kellaway and
Percy Keown)
1864
25.3 x 19.7 cm
V&A: PH.332–1981

The Mariner's Wife
1864–5
25 x 20 cm
V&A: PH.333–1981

Madonna and Child
1864
25 x 20 cm
V&A: PH.334–1981

The Shunammite Woman and her dead Son
1865
27.2 x 22.6 cm
V&A: PH.335–1981

Daughters of Jerusalem
1865
34.5 x 26.2 cm
V&A: PH.336–1981

Shepherds Keeping Watch By Night
1865–6
29 x 23 cm
V&A: PH.337–1981

Madonna and Child
1864–5
23 x 20 cm
V&A: PH.338–1981

Madonna and Child
1864–5
18 x 13 cm
V&A: PH.339-1981

Madonna and Two Children
1864
25 x 20 cm
V&A: PH.340–1981

Madonna and Two Children
1864
23.5 x 18 cm
V&A: PH.341–1981

Mary Hillier
1864–5
25.4 x 19.7 cm
V&A: PH.342–1981

The three Marys
1864
24.2 x 20.6 cm
V&A: PH.343–1981

Group (Mary Ryan, Mary Hillier and Mary Kellaway)
1864
25 x 20.3 cm
V&A: PH.344–1981

Madonna and Two
Children
1864
23.7 x 19.8 cm
V&A: PH.345–1981

Mary Hillier
1864–6
25.5 x 19.8 cm
V&A: PH.346–1981

The Salutation
1864
25.5 x 19.9 cm
V&A: PH.347–1981

Trust
1865
19 x 15 cm
V&A: PH.348–1981

Sister Spirits
1865
35 x 28.5 cm
V&A: PH.349–1981

Group (Percy Keown
and unknown girl)
1864
29.1 x 22.6 cm
V&A: PH.350–1981

Christiana
Fraser-Tytler
1864–5
26.4 x 22.2 cm
V&A: PH.351–1981

The grandmother
1865
30 x 21 cm
V&A: PH.352–1981

Group (Alice DuCane
and unknown woman)
1864–5
24.3 x 19.2 cm
V&A: PH.353–1981

Unknown Woman
c.1874
37.5 x 27 cm
V&A: PH.354–1981

*A Sibyl after
the manner of
Michelangelo*
1864
28.5 x 22.5 cm
V&A: PH.355–1981

Charlotte Norman
c.1864–6
25.2 x 20 cm
V&A: PH.356–1981

May Prinsep
1864–6

23.5 x 18 cm

V&A: PH.357–1981

Possibly by Oscar Gustaf
Rejlander, possibly in
collaboration with, and/or
printed by, Julia Margaret
Cameron
Unknown Woman (May
Prinsep?)
c. 1863

20.5 x 16.5 cm

V&A: PH.358–1981

Unknown man
1864–6

22 x 20 cm

Originally catalogued as
204–1969 and thought to be
Charles Keene

V&A: PH.359–1981

William Creedly
1864–6

30 x 16 cm

Originally catalogued as
229–1969

V&A: PH.360–1981

Julia Jackson
1867

31 x 26 cm

Originally catalogued as
230–1969

V&A: PH.361–1981

Hardinge Hay
Cameron
May 1864

29 x 23 cm

V&A: PH.362–1981

Joy
1864

26 x 20 cm

V&A: PH.363–1981

The Minstrel Group
1866

34.5 x 28.5 cm

V&A: PH.240–1982

The Turtle Doves
1864

18.8 x 14.4 cm

V&A: PH.241–1982

Jacob and Rachel
1864

25.7 x 21.5 cm

V&A: PH.242–1982

Hosanna
1865

29.2 x 22.4 cm

V&A: PH.243–1982

Hosanna
1865

29.5 x 22.6 cm

V&A: PH.244–1982

Hosanna
1865
29 x 22.4 cm
V&A: PH.245–1982

The grandmother
1865
25 x 22 cm
V&A: PH.246–1982

Paul and Virginia
1864
26 x 20 cm
V&A: PH.247–1982

Diana
c.1864–6
26 x 20 cm
V&A: PH.248–1982

The Neapolitan
1866
30.5 x 26 cm
V&A: PH.249–1982

The Neapolitan
1866
8.5 x 6.3 cm
V&A: PH.250–1982

The Infant Bridal
1864
24.5 x 19.4 cm
V&A: PH.251–1982

Zoe/Maid of Athens
1866
32.0 x 27.2 cm
V&A: PH.252–1982

Light and Love
June 1865
25 x 21 cm
V&A: PH.253–1982

Madonna and Two
Children
1864
24 x 19 cm
V&A: PH.254–1982

Lady Elcho/
A Dantesque Vision
1865
27.3 x 22.5 cm
V&A: PH.255–1982

Marianne North
1877
28.3 x 23.3 cm
V&A: PH.256–1982

May Prinsep
October 1870

34.9 x 27.6 cm

V&A: PH.257–1982

Oscar Gustaf Rejlander,
possibly in collaboration
with Julia Margaret
Cameron; printed by Julia
Margaret Cameron
Kate Dore
c.1862

19.6 x 15 cm

V&A: PH.258–1982

Possibly by Oscar Gustaf
Rejlander, possibly in
collaboration with, and/or
printed by, Julia Margaret
Cameron
Unknown Woman
c.1863

16.5 x 12.5 cm

V&A: PH.259–1982

Possibly by Oscar
Gustaf Rejlander, pos-
sibly in collaboration
with, and/or printed
by, Julia Margaret
Cameron
Unknown Woman
c.1864

V&A: PH.260–1982

**Bequeathed by
Guy Little
1953**

Possibly by Oscar Gustaf
Rejlander, possibly in
collaboration with, and/or
printed by, Julia Margaret
Cameron
*The Idylls of the Village or
The Idols of the Villages*
c.1863

16 x 10.8 cm

Inscribed by JMC: *The Marys at
the Well/of Fresh Water/A Pastoral
Gem/for the Signor* [circled]

V&A: PH.261–1982

Sadness
27 February 1864

13.7 x 9.6 cm

V&A: S.133:183–2007

**Given by Mrs
Whiteley
1957**

**Given by
Window & Grove
1963**

Unknown Woman
1868–72

34 x 25 cm

V&A: 232–1957

Hypatia
1868

30.5 x 24.5 cm

V&A: 1141–1963

Henry Taylor
10 October 1867

34 x 28 cm

V&A: 1142–1963

Alfred Tennyson
May 1865

A. Tennyson [facsimile
signature]

25.2 x 20.1 cm

V&A: 1143–1963

*John Frederick
William Herschel*
April 1867

32.1 x 24.2 cm

V&A: 1144–1963

**Acquired from Mr
and Mrs Ronald
Lindsay
1972**

Possibly a collaboration between Cameron and her son
"The Angel in the House", 1871

*Inscribed by JMC: Autotype taken
from Photograph from the Life*

*by Henry Herschel Hay Cameron
Freshwater 1871*

V&A: E.2309–1997

**Bequeathed by
John Nevinson
1986**

Unknown girl
1865–6

30.9 x 25.4 cm

V&A: E.2743–1990

Annie Chinery
Cameron
1869–70

34.5 x 24.3 cm

V&A: E.2744–1990

*After the Manner of
the Elgin Marbles*
1867

28.8 x 24.1 cm

V&A: E.2745–1990

Henry Taylor
1864, printed later,
probably before 1884

Collotype

21.8 x 17.4 cm

V&A: E.2746–1990

Alfred Tennyson
3 June 1869, printed
later, probably
before 1884

Collotype

29.8 x 24.2 cm

V&A: E.2747–1990

George Frederic Watts
1864, printed later,
probably before 1884

Collotype

21.4 x 18.3 cm

V&A: E.2748–1990

The Angel at the Tomb
1870, printed later,
probably before 1884

Collotype

28.8 x 21.3 cm

V&A: E.2749–1990

A Study of the Cenci
1870, printed later,
probably before 1884

Collotype

30.3 x 23.4 cm

V&A: E.2750–1990

Florence Anson
1866, printed later,
probably before 1884

Collotype

26.2 x 23 cm

V&A: E.2751–1990

*The Mountain Nymph
Sweet Liberty*
June 1866, printed
later, probably
before 1884

Collotype

29.4 x 22.3 cm

V&A: E.2752–1990

Rosalba
1867, printed later,
probably before 1884

Collotype

30.5 x 23.5 cm

V&A: E.2753–1990

Henry John Stedman
Cotton
May 1867

28.6 x 23.3 cm

V&A: E.2754–1990

**Given by Mark
Haworth–Booth
1994**

Mrs. Herbert Duckworth,
from the portfolio *The
Golden Age of British
Photography*
1867, printed 1985

Photogravure

34.5 x 26.2 cm

V&A: E.89–1994

Henry Herschel Hay Cameron
Julia Margaret Cameron
c.1870
25 x 21.5 cm
V&A: E.1217–2000

Long-suffering
1864
From the series *Fruits of the Spirit*
28.9 x 22.6 cm
V&A: E.1218–2000

Joy
c.1864
From the series *Fruits of the Spirit*
25.6 x 20 cm
V&A: E.1219–2000

Gentleness
1864
From the series *Fruits of the Spirit*
29.1 x 21.1 cm
V&A: E.1220–2000

Love
1864
From the series *Fruits of the Spirit*
26.3 x 20.7 cm
V&A: E.1221–2000

Faith
1864
From the series *Fruits of the Spirit*
27.9 x 21.3 cm
V&A: E.1222–2000

Goodness
1864
From the series *Fruits of the Spirit*
28.5 x 22.2 cm
V&A: E.1223–2000

Meekness
1864
From the series *Fruits of the Spirit*
29.4 x 22.2 cm
V&A: E.1224–2000

Peace also known as *La Madonna della Ricordanza/Kept in the heart*
1864
From the series *Fruits of the Spirit*
28.9 x 21.4 cm
V&A: E.1225–2000

Temperance
1864
From the series *Fruits of the Spirit*
28.6 x 22.3 cm
V&A: E.1226–2000

Appendix II
Letters from Julia Margaret Cameron to Henry Cole

The following five letters from Julia Margaret Cameron to Henry Cole are in the collection of the National Art Library at the Victoria and Albert Museum.

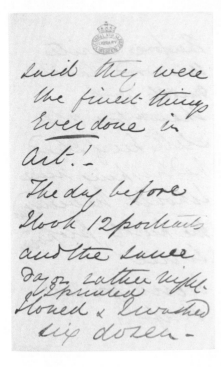

A

Little Holland House
May 20 Saturday [1865]

My Dear Mr Cole

I have real pleasure in telling
you that Mr. Watts thinks
my Photograph of you
"Extremely fine" I hope to
tone & wash tonight after

B

a day's <u>most</u> arduous work I
really fear even my energies
breaking down with the
work of today. All yesty
[yesterday] I took studies of
Lady Elcho & Lord Elcho

C

said they were the finest
things <u>Ever done</u> in Art!
The day before I took 12
portraits and the same day
or rather night I printed I
toned & I washed six dozen –

D

therefore I write this word
standing midst work. Thank
your Wife & tell her if I had
had breathing time I <u>should</u>
have enjoyed the kindly
proposed soirée
I send you my Portfolio

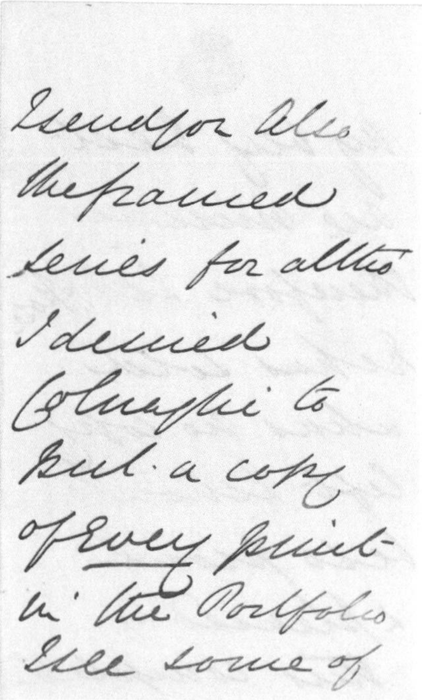

[Handwritten letter, panel E]

I send you also
the framed
series for altho
I desired
Colnaghi to
put a copy
of _Every_ print
in the Portfolio
I see some of

E

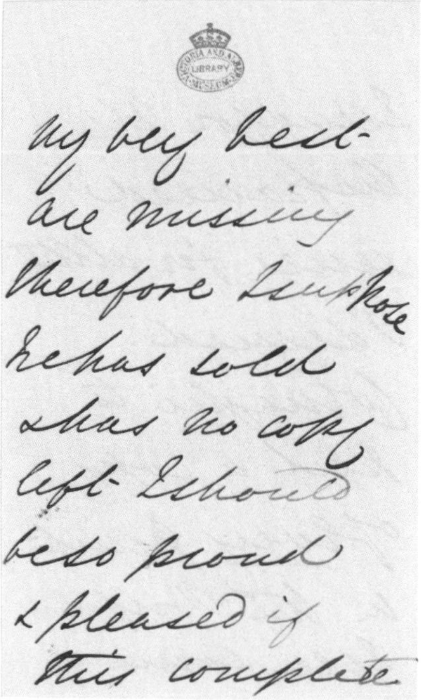

[Handwritten letter, panel F]

my very best
are missing
therefore I suppose
he has sold
& has no copy
left I should
be so proud
& pleased if
this complete

F

E

I send you also the framed
series for altho I desired
Colnaghi to put a copy of
Every print in the Portfolio
I see some of

F

my very best are missing
therefore I suppose he
has sold & has no copy
left I should be so proud &
pleased if this complete

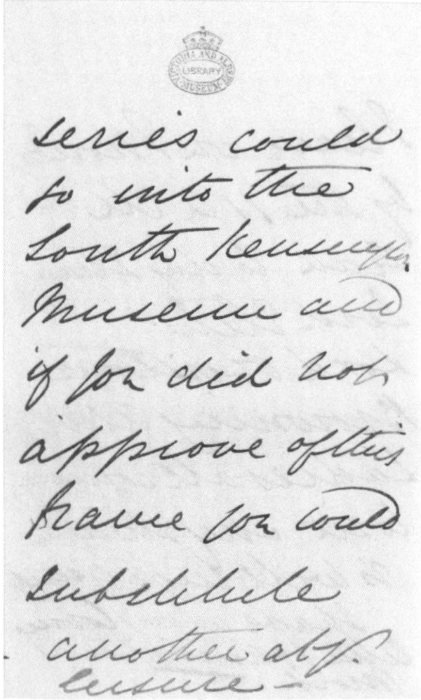

[Handwritten letter, panel G]

series could
go into the
South Kensing.
Museum and
if you did not
approve of this
frame you could
substitute
another at y.
leisure –

G

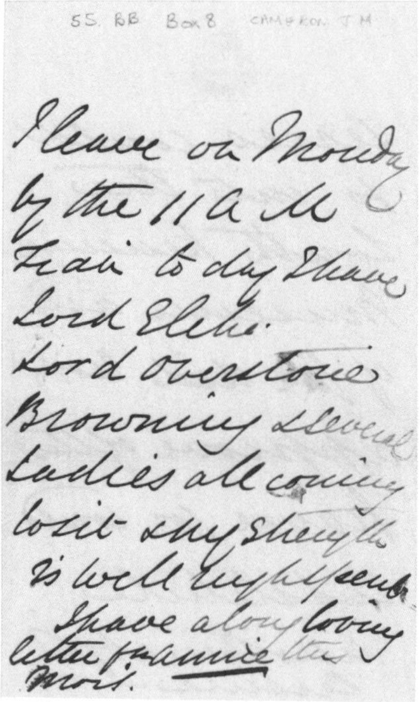

[Handwritten letter, panel H]

I leave on Monday
by the 11 A M
Train to day I have
Lord Elcho.
Lord Overstone
Browning & several
Ladies all coming
to sit & my strength
is well nigh spent.
I have a long loving
letter for annie this
mail.

H

G

series could go into the South
Kensington Museum and if
you did not approve of this
frame you could substitute
another at yr. leisure –

H

I leave on Monday by the
11am Train today I have
Lord Elcho Lord Overstone
Browning & several Ladies
all coming to sit & my
strength is well nigh spent.
I have a long loving letter for
Annie this mail.

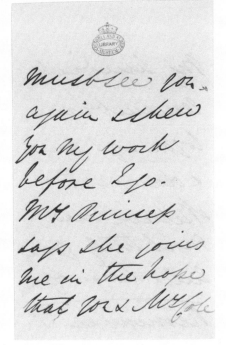

I

My kindest remembrances
to you yr Wife & daughters
& Believe me Most truly
yours
Julia Margaret Cameron
Remember I

J

must see you again & shew
you my work before I go.
Mrs Prinsep says she joins
me in the hope that you &
Mrs Cole

K

& your daughters will come
to our shady! Garden here
tomorrow afternoon
<u>Yes?</u>
JMC

21 February 1866

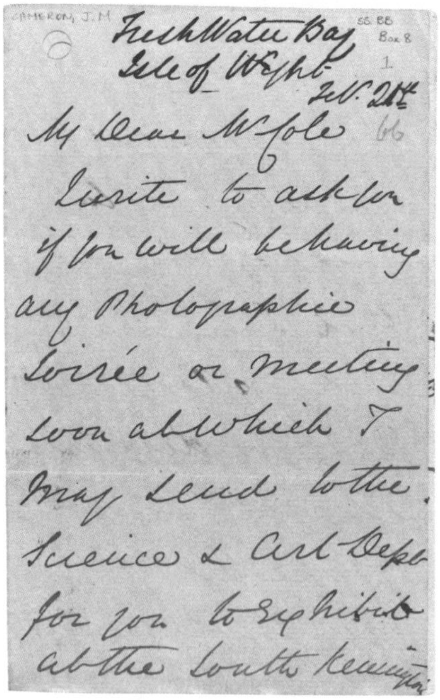

A

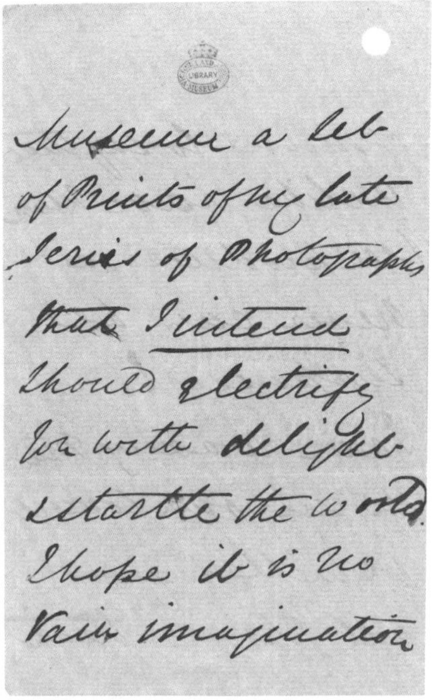

B

A

Fresh Water Bay
Isle Of Wight
Feb 21st [1866]

My Dear Mr Cole

I write to ask you if you will be having any Photographic Soirée or meeting soon at which I may send to the Science & Art Dept. for you to exhibit at the South Kensington

B

Museum a set of Prints of my late series of Photographs that I intend should electrify you with delight & startle the world. I hope it is no vain imagination

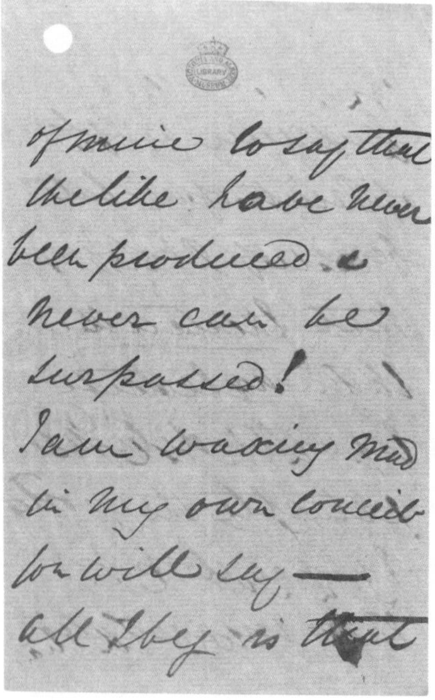

C

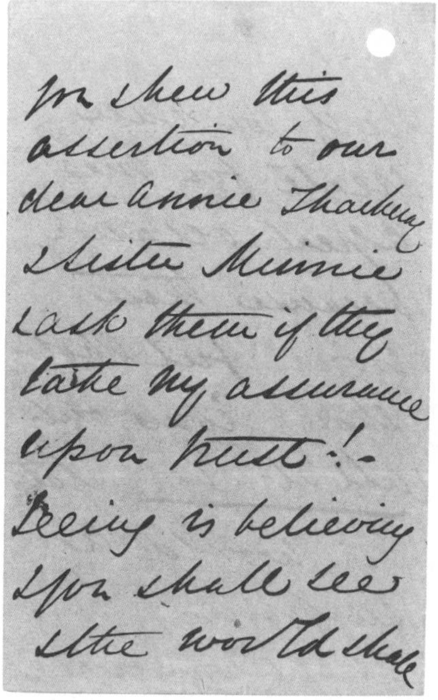

D

C

of mine to say that the like have never been produced & never can be surpassed! I am waxing mad in my own conceit you will say –
All I beg is that

D

you show this assertion to our dear Annie Thackeray & sister Minnie & ask them if they take my assurance upon trust! Seeing is believing & you shall see & the world shall

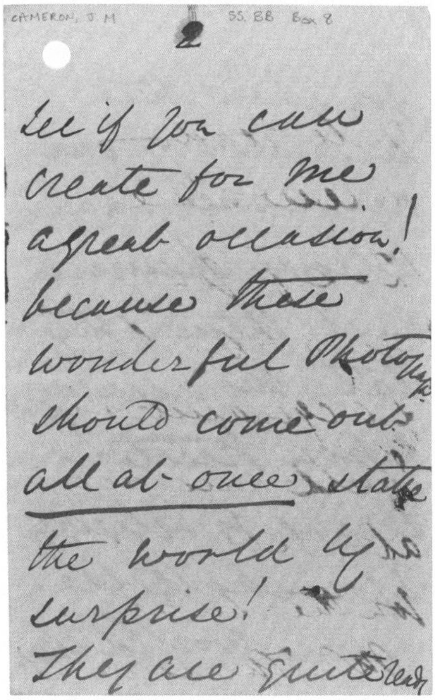

E

F

E

see if you can create for
me a great occasion!
because these wonderful
Photographs should come
out all at once & take the
world by surprise! They are
quite ready

F

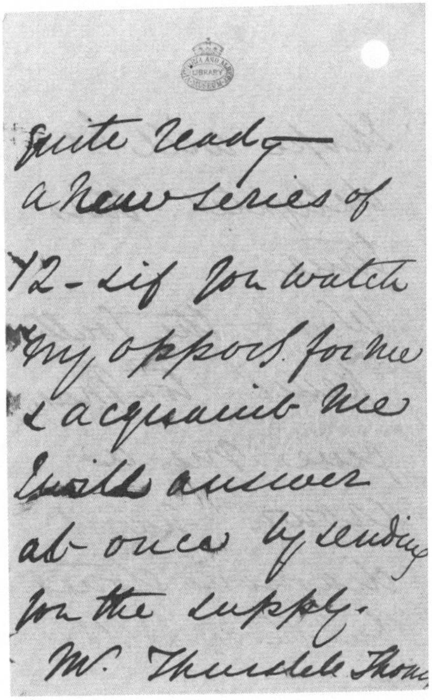

quite ready – A new series of
12 & if you watch my opport
[opportunities] for me &
acquaint me I will answer
at once by sending you
the supply. Mr. Thurston
Thompson

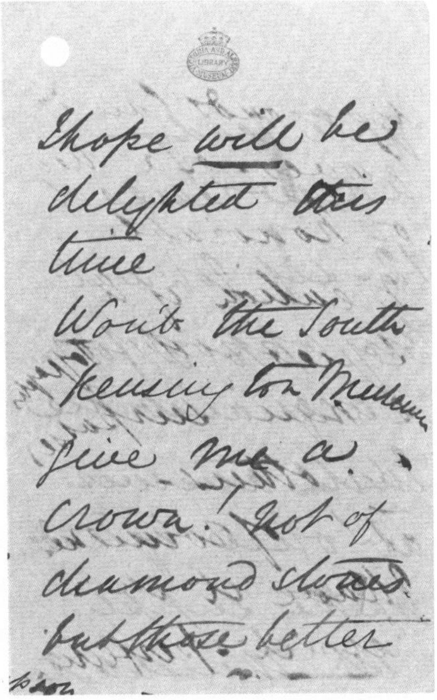

G

H

G

I hope will be delighted
this time.
Won't the South Kensington
Museum give me a crown!
Not of diamond stones but
those better

H

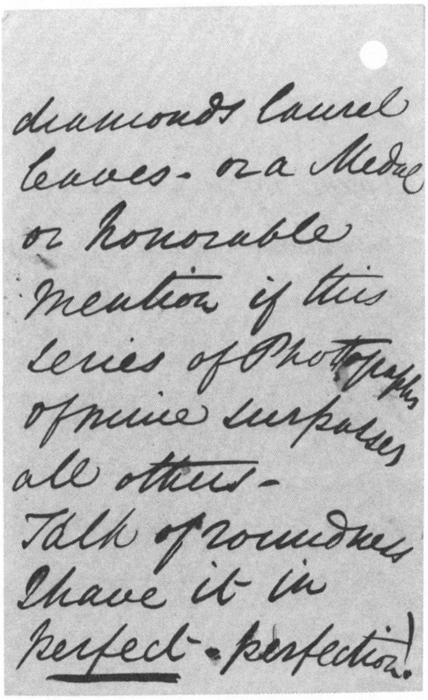

diamonds laurel leaves –
or a Medal or honorable
[sic] mention if this series
of Photographs of mine
surpasses all others – Talk
of roundness I have it in
perfect perfection!

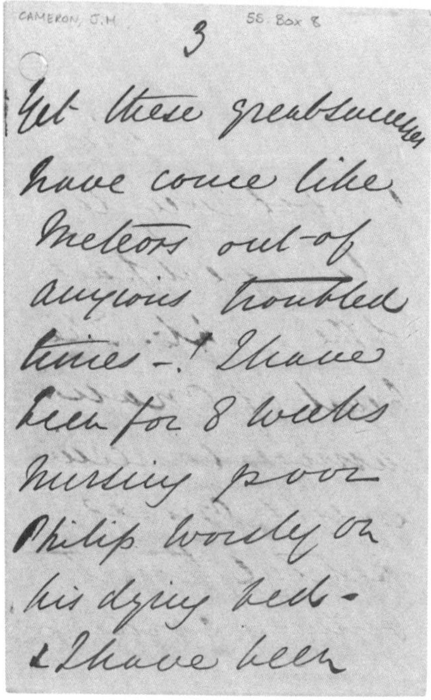

I

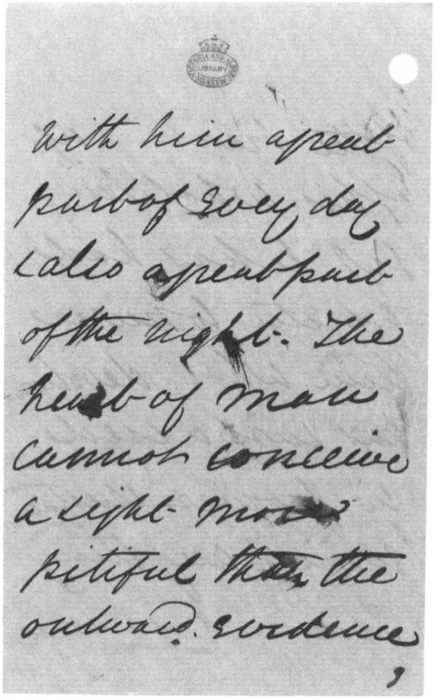

J

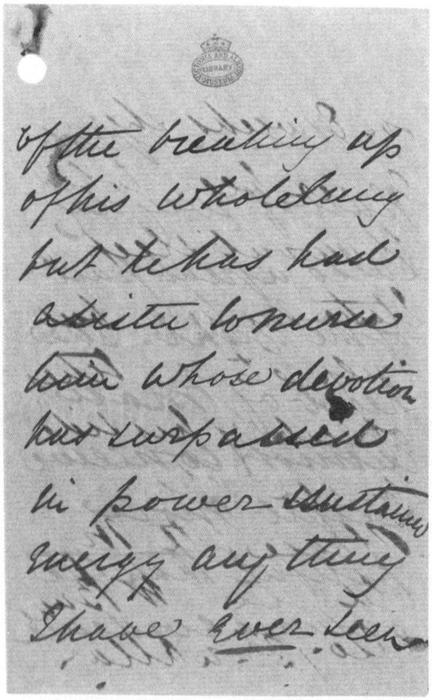

K

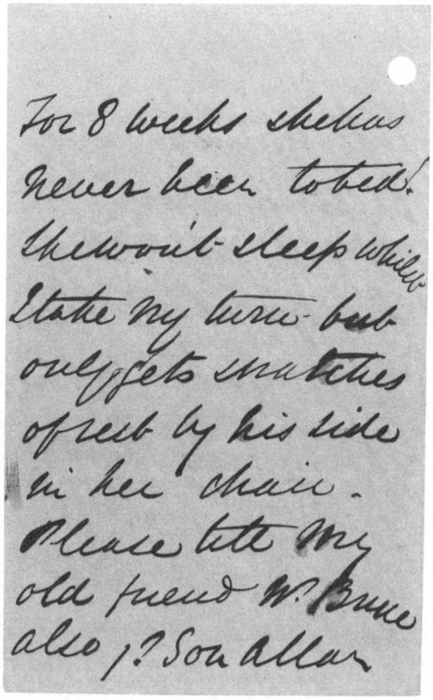

L

I

Yet these great successes have come like meteors out of anxious troubled times -! I have been for 8 weeks nursing poor Philip Worsley on his dying bed – & I have been

J

with him a great part of every day & also a great part of the night. The heart of man cannot conceive a sight more pitiful than the outward evidence

K

of the breaking up of his whole being but he has had a sister to nurse him whose devotion has surpassed in power & sustained energy anything I have <u>ever</u> seen

L

For 8 weeks she has never been to bed! She won't sleep whilst I take my turn but only gets snatches of rest by his side in her chair. Please tell my old friend Mr. Bruce also yr. Son Allan [*sic*]

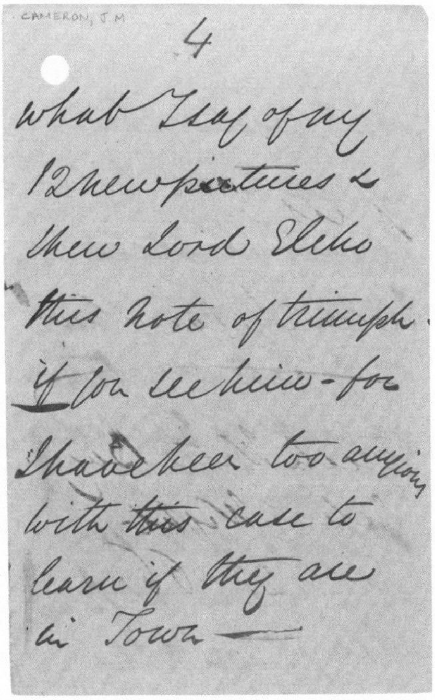

M

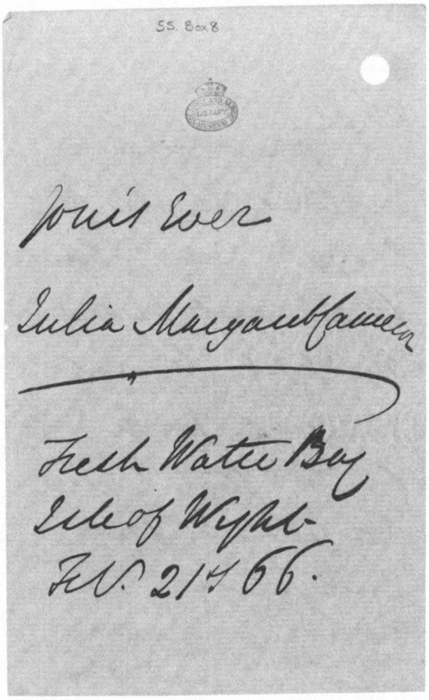

what I say of my 12 new
pictures & show Lord Elcho
this note of triumph if you
see him – for I have been too
anxious with this case to
learn if they are in Town –

N

Yours Ever
Julia Margaret Cameron
Fresh Water Bay
Isle of Wight
IW 21766

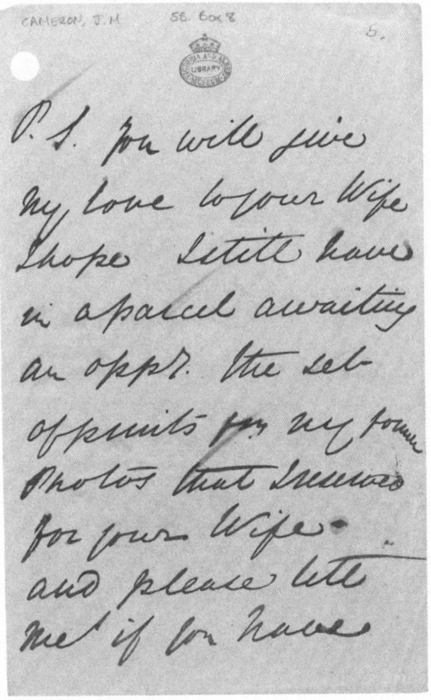

O

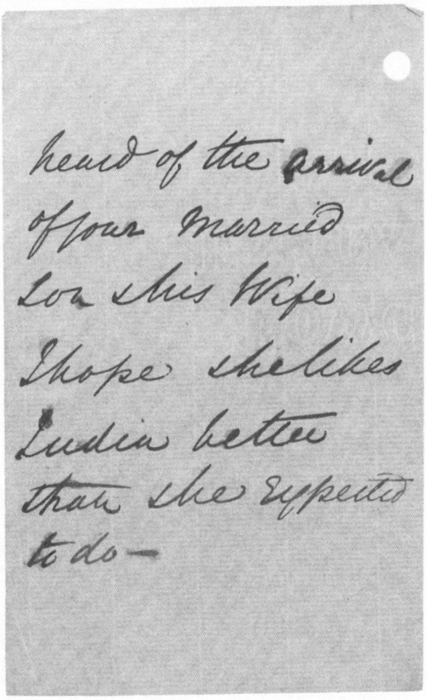

P.S. You will give my love to
your Wife I hope I still have
in a parcel awaiting an oppt.
[opportunity] the set of
prints frm [from] my former
Photos that I reserved for
your Wife – and please tell
me if you have

P

heard of the arrival of your
married son & his Wife I
hope she likes India better
than she expected to do –

M

N

O

P

A

B

C

D

A

Fresh Water Bay
Isle of Wight
April 7th [18]68

My Dear Mr Cole

In the hurry of our departure
from London yesterday morn
(and the anxiety of getting my
Husband gently away without
his sharing in the hurry) your
parcel of Mr. Pouncey's work
was put by mistake with our
luggage I now return it to you
with all possible care & speed
by this same post.

B

Pray thank your Son for
so kindly bringing it. It is
beautifully & carefully done
but I cannot say that I think
the artistic character of photography is preserved. I should
like to hear the opinion of Mr
Watts & other artists on this
subject. I think as you say for
House Decoration & for things
seen from afar this process

C

ought to have a brilliant
success but for anything
so delicate as a portrait the
shinning glazed surface
destroys the pleasure by
giving a sticking plaster look
& I think that even in oil
paintings any thick coating
of Varnish is a great injury to
the effect. It is the dull quiet

D

surface of a photograph however rich in tone & tint it may
be, that constitutes I think
the harmony of the work &
therefore I have not answered
Lord Dufferin's letter to me:
I did not wish to say I did not
like Mr. Pouncey's plan of
rendering Portraits, but
I could not say I did.
I asked your son to Exhibit
to you the little gallery of my
work in your Museum which
I left there

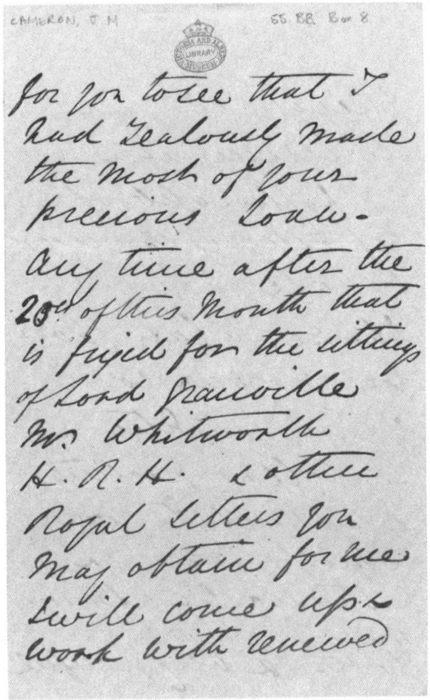

for you to see that I
had zealously made
the most of your
precious loan -
Any time after the
20th of this month that
is fixed for the sittings
of Lord Granville
Mr. Whitworth
H.R.H. & other
Royal Sitters you
may obtain for me
I will come up &
work with renewed

E

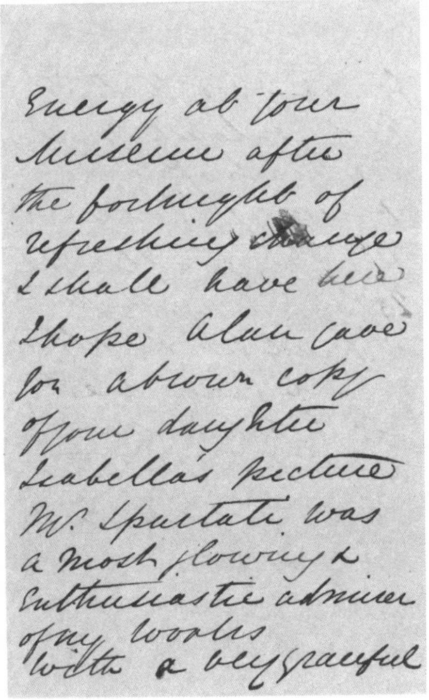
energy at your
Museum after
the fortnight of
refreshing change
I shall have here
I hope Alan gave
you a brown copy
of your daughter
Isabella's picture
Mr. Spartali was
a most glowing &
enthusiastic admirer
of my works
with a very graceful

F

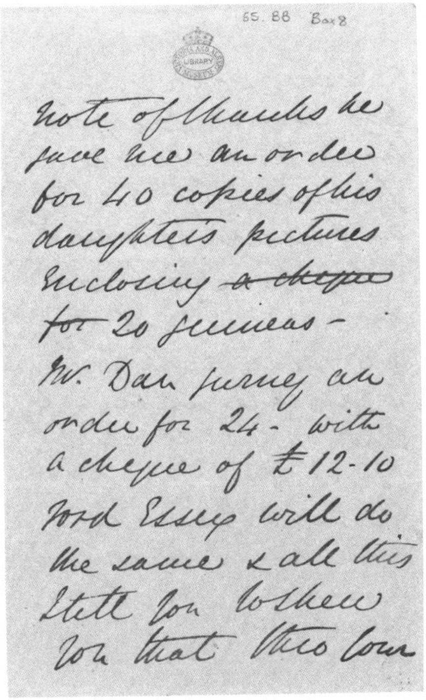

note of thanks he
gave me an order
for 40 copies of his
daughter's pictures
enclosing ~~a cheque~~
for 20 guineas -
Mr. Dan Gurney an
order for 24 - with
a cheque of £12-10
Lord Essex will do
the same & all this
I tell you to shew
you that thro your

G

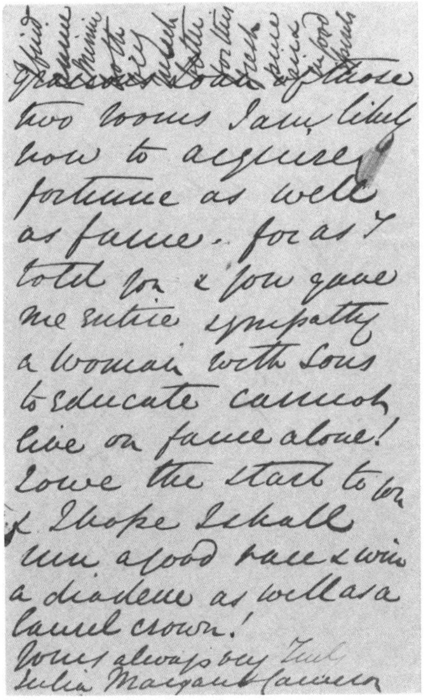
I find Annie & Minnie both very much better for this fresh pure air & in good spirits
gracious loan of those
two rooms I am likely
now to acquire
fortune as well
as fame - for as I
told you & you gave
me entire sympathy
a woman with sons
to educate cannot
live on fame alone!
I owe the start to you
& I hope I shall
run a good race & win
a diadem as well as a
laurel crown!
Yours always very Truly
Julia Margaret Cameron

H

E

for you to see that I had zealously made the most of your precious loan.
Any time after the 20th of this month that is fixed for the sittings of Lord Granville Mr. Whitworth H.R.H. & other Royal Sitters you may obtain for me I will come up & work with renewed

F

energy at your Museum after the fortnight of refreshing change I shall have here.
I hope Alan gave you a brown copy of your daughter Isabella's picture
Mr. Spartali was a most glowing & enthusiastic admirer of my works with a very graceful

G

note of thanks he gave me an order for 40 copies of his daughter's pictures enclosing ~~a cheque for~~ 20 guineas – Mr. Dan Gurney an order for 24 – with a cheque of £12.10. Lord Essex will do the same & all this I tell you to shew you that thro your

H

gracious loan of those two rooms I am likely now to acquire fortune as well as fame, for as I told you & you gave me entire sympathy a woman with sons to educate cannot live on fame alone! I owe the start to you & I hope I shall run a good race & win a diadem as well as a laurel crown!
Yours always very Truly
Julia Margaret Cameron

I find Annie & Minnie both very much better for this fresh pure air & in good spirits

A

B

C

D

A

Fresh Water Bay
June 12th [18]69
I[sle] of W.[ight]

My Dear Mr Cole

I have so perpetually remembered all yr. helping kindness & ever friendly hand to me in the earlier years of my Art that I delight in now sending you four of my latest works as my grateful gift to you including the very latest of all, my last portrait of Alfred Tennyson (not yet published)

B

which I think you will agree with me in feeling is a National Treasure of immense Value* – next to the living speaking man must ever stand this Portrait of him, quite the most

*I send a copy for the much loved Annie & Minnie which you will give them issue of for me won't you [at top of page]

C

faithful & most noble Portrait of him existing – Surely this Portrait ought to be engraved for altho' I can secure thro' my own care the durability & permanence of my print, I can alas do nothing to make durable the far more

D

precious original negative. The chemicals supplied to me for this are beyond my power & prove fatally perishable. 45 of my most precious negatives this year have perished thro the fault of Collodion or Varnish supplied: both or either destroy the film that holds the picture – You will see in the Dream the commencement of this cruel calamity – also in the Guardian Angel – which has over taken 45 of my Gems – a honey comb crack extending over the picture appearing at any moment & beyond any power to arrest

E

F

G

H

E

I went up to the Photographic meeting & put this question before 50 or 60 men & every one of the most practised Photographers gave me a different reason for this fatal accident to negatives all were in error as no reason explained why all the negatives of my first four years are as perfect as the day on which

F

they were done – a change in the manufacture of Varnish & Collodion only explains the change to me – but I see two grand things to remember now First to print as actively as I can whilst my precious negative is yet good

G

Secondly to try to get the Portraits I have taken of our greatest men engraved Mr. Layard promised enthusiastically to help on my cause & my friends in Photography Think with a kind generous head, what you can do for me – & will you?

H

Are there no Schools of art for which you can now send me orders – Is there no corner of the S.[outh] K[ensington] Museum where you can install me – You know I have my Gold Medal – but even now after five years of toil, ardent patient persisting toil I have not yet by one Hundred Pounds recovered the money I have spent

E [REPRISE]

I won't tire you more I called twice when I was in London for a fortnight beginning of last month With my love to your Wife and to Allan [sic] and to all yours ev. Julia Margaret Cameron

A

B

C

D

A

30 Albemarle St
Dec 24 [1872]
My Dear Sir Henry Cole

Will you or your Son Allan [sic]
take pity on my ignorance
& instruct me speedily on
these points
I have taken great pains to
have my latest and I

B

think almost my best photographs ready and framed for
the Vienna Exhibition
I applied for Space months
ago and I was told I should
be duly informed of all
particulars

C

I asked for two & a half
square metres I am very
modest as to the number of
Photographs I send
When am I to send what is
now ready – ? and where am
I to send my Photographs?
in what form too? in ~~square~~
packing cases – Can I be
saved Expenses –

D

Does not that Princely Mr.
Wallace extend his bounty
to all works of art including
Photography
I am ill, as Annie Thackeray
~~will~~ may have told you for
five weeks I have been in one
room. I am just emerging &
flying homewards so that I am

A [REPRISE]

eager for an answer and I
know your kindness needs
no fanning into action yrs
very truly Julia Margaret
Cameron

Dec 24 '72 Clarke's Private
Hotel 30 Albemarle St

Acknowledgements

It has been a privilege and a pleasure to inhabit the world of Julia Margaret Cameron and I am grateful to the numerous individuals who ventured there with me over the past two years.

At the V&A, Erika Lederman provided brilliant research assistance and delighted in each discovery as much as I did. James Sutton and Christopher Marsden helped unlock secrets hidden in the V&A Archives. Bill Sherman, Katherine Elliott and the rest of the Research Department gave me a supportive and stimulating working environment. Conservators Simon Fleury, Boris Pretzel and Jane Rutherston helped prolong the physical wellbeing of Cameron's work. Thank you to Zoe Louizos and Ross Head for the calm and competent organisation of an extensive international tour and gorgeous V&A exhibition, and to Jo Ani for helping secure a sponsor. For their on-going support I thank my colleagues in the Photographs Section: Martin Barnes, Susanna Brown and Bronwen Colquhoun, as well as Briony Carlin, Zein Khalifa and Lisa Springer. I thank Mark Evans and Liz Miller for contributing their paintings and prints expertise. Finally, I gratefully acknowledge the previous investigations of the V&A's Cameron collection by Mark Haworth-Booth, Magda Keaney and Elisa Canossa.

The following colleagues, near and far, generously shared information about and granted access to works by Julia Margaret Cameron: Barbara Diener at the Art Institute of Chicago; Nichole Fazio-Veigel on behalf of the Bodleian Library; Jennifer Bescoby and Alison Wright at the British Museum; Margaretta Frederick at the Delaware Art Museum; Rachel Flynn at Dimbola Museum and Galleries; James Hervey-Bathurst and Hazel Lein at Eastnor Castle; Julian Cox at the Fine Arts Museums of San Francisco; Jessica Johnston at the George Eastman House; Leslie Cozzi at the Hammer Museum; Jessica S. McDonald at the Harry Ransom Center; Anita Louise Bracalente and Nan Brewer at the Indiana University Art Museum; Karen Hellman at the J. Paul Getty Museum; Hans P. Kraus; Claire McHugh and Daniel Robbins at the Leighton House Museum; Michael P. Mattis; Thomas Galifot at the Musée d'Orsay; Kristen Gresh at the Museum of Fine Arts, Boston; Rebecca Smith at the National Media Museum; Shannon Perich at the National Museum of American History; Georgia Atienza, Ruth Slaney and Helen Trompeteler at the National Portrait Gallery; Victoria Olsen at NYU; and Marlaine Des Champs at the Special Collections and Archives of Union College. For facilitating loans and reproductions, my particular thanks go to Eve Watson at the Royal Society of Arts, Nicholas Tromans at the Watts Gallery, and Polly Fleury, Hope Kingsley and Ella Naef at the Wilson Centre for Photography. Thank you also to Jane and Michael Wilson.

I am grateful to Malcolm Daniel, Colin Ford, Juliet Hacking and the late Violet Hamilton for sharing their Cameron expertise with me at various stages of the project. I also thank Mark Osterman and France Scully Osterman for helping me make sense of Cameron's process, Michael Pritchard for providing the dates of her Photographic Society membership and Gabriele Rossi Rognoni for identifying the musical instruments in her photographs. Above all, I am indebted to Joanne Lukitsh for her generous and extensive feedback.

For their help producing this beautiful book I thank my colleagues in V&A Publishing: Mark Eastment, Nina Jacobson, Zara Anvari, Rosemary Brook-Hart and Leigh Mitnick. Special thanks go to Tom Windross for his good-humoured professionalism. At MACK, I thank Michael Mack for his enthusiasm, Grégoire Pujade-Lauraine for an elegant design, and Liz Jobey for her sharp editorial eye.

This book and the exhibition it accompanies would not have been possible without the support of the Bern Schwartz Family Foundation. Like Julia Margaret Cameron, Bern Schwartz took up photography late in life, and, like Cameron, he exhibited at Colnaghi. I am grateful to the members of the Schwartz family for such a fitting and generous grant and give my warm thanks to Anne Varick Lauder for bringing us together.

Alex Paseau helped me fathom Victorian currency and the difference between accidents and mistakes. I thank him for his support and patience, along with that of Athena, who would have made a perfect subject for Julia Margaret Cameron.

Marta Weiss
Curator, Photographs
Victoria and Albert Museum

This book accompanied the exhibition
Julia Margaret Cameron, organised by
the Victoria and Albert Museum, London.

Art Gallery of New South Wales, Sydney
13 August 2015 – 25 October 2015

Victoria and Albert Museum, London
28 November 2015 – 21 February 2016

At the Victoria and Albert Museum, the exhibition was
supported by The Bern Schwartz Family Foundation.
This donation was made possible by the American
Friends of the V&A.

Second printing published by MACK

Design Grégoire Pujade-Lauraine
Printing EBS

© 2018 MACK
V&A images and text © 2018 Victoria and Albert Museum, London

MACK
mackbooks.co.uk

ISBN 978-1-910164-29-7